The Column Rule
Rockland People, Rockland Places

About the Illustrations

The photographs on the cover of this book and at the beginning of each section were taken by the author, Arthur H. Gunther 3rd.

Early in his career at The Journal News, Gunther learned newspaper photography and was soon signed on as a full-time photographer for the paper. Later moving over to the editing side of The Journal News, he eventually became the Editorial Page Editor. However, he continues to take and exhibit photographs.

The Column Rule
Rockland People, Rockland Places

By

Arthur H. Gunther 3rd

The Historical Society of Rockland County
New City, N.Y.

The Historical Society of Rockland County

Library of Congress Cataloguing-in-Publication Data

Gunther, Arthur H. (Arthur Henry), 1942-
    The column rule : Rockland people, Rockland Places / by Arthur H. Gunther.
    p. cm.
    Includes index.
    ISBN 0-911183-51-5 (hardcover : alk.paper) – ISBN 0-91183-52-3 (pbk. : alk.paper)
    1. Rockland County (N.Y.)—Social life and customs—Anecdotes. 2. Rockland County
    N.Y.)—Biography—Anecdotes. 3. Rockland County (N.Y.)—History—Anecdotes.
    I. Title.

F127.R6G86 2006
974.7'2—dc22   2006043458

The essays in this book are reprinted with the permission of The Journal News,
for which they were originally written and in which they were published.
This publication has been made possible, in part, by a grant from the Gannett Foundation.

The Historical Society of Rockland County
20 Zukor Road
New City, N.Y. 10956
Telephone: 845-634-9629
E-mail: info@rocklandhistory.org

Contents

Foreword vii

Preface x

Sections

    Rockland People 1

    Rockland Places 71

    Rockland History 97

    Various Themes 159

Index 219

Foreword

In high school many, many years ago, I came totally unprepared one day for the afternoon history class and when my teacher hit me with a question I conjured up an answer out of the whole cloth of nothingness.

"Jobson," the teacher asked sternly, "what is the price of eggs in China?" The class tittered. Her well-crafted question sank in with a twinge.

When I became The Journal News Editorial Page editor, I well remembered that teacher's nip at my heels and I vowed I would never write a meaningless what-is-the-price-of-eggs-in-China editorial.

Moreover, I have never found one in Arthur H. Gunther's editorials or something like that in his "The Column Rule." His writing attains immediacy and relevancy and identifies with Rockland County just as its landmarks do.

His columns also reflect the changes that came—and are still coming—with the building of The Bridge. As time is counted, these changes did not come over a great spread of years. Regardless, as the last century wore down and the new one came in, they amounted to specific eras, short as they were.

They engaged Arthur's life in Rockland as a free spirited and imaginative boy and as a working man with a family who shelled out for the mortgage, the utilities and the insurance—all of them the heavy load of suburban "progress." I knew that heavy load when I inhabited a brick ranch in New City. County growth, taxes and demands for expanded municipal services occupied me on the editorial page, but I never had the knowledge of the workings of suburban obligations and finances that Arthur does.

His editorials and columns on the demands suburbia makes on its people have an authority I never possessed. Knowledgeable suburbanites have a real friend in Arthur.

So do the ecology-minded, for Arthur is a robust companion of nature and its local wonders. In one of his columns about the frenzy of life and how nature often steps in to cool the pot, he refers to "the fresh morning, with the smell of summer's humidity and the dew that glistens as a bright sun hits the dark green grass."

In this column Arthur makes mention of a geographical location in Rockland and it reminds me of his "Traveling Editorial Page" when he finds something in the nooks and crannies of the county that needs attention.

Another of his columns, "Walking on the Boulevard," is especially enjoyable for me because I know the location mentioned from the rides my parents and I took around Rockland on a summer's night, and also because I am acquainted with another, larger site near the apartment of my maternal grandmother's sister in the Bronx.

Arthur's "Boulevard" is described by him as "the one-mile stretch from Spring Valley to Hillcrest, from downtown to the Hillcrest Hotel." The description of this section, where my father on our rides always drove as slowly as possible, is one of the finest I have read about ethnic America and its roots.

Arthur notes that the "Boulevard" was not just a sidewalk. "It was a public square, where men discussed politics and women their homes, children and husbands. It was decision ground, where futures were charted and dreams were verbalized, where mothers talked of lawyers and doctors-to-be."

Then Arthur makes a big, sweeping statement that justly brings up, however small the scale was, the immigration that gave Rockland its first phase of diversity: the "Boulevard represented "Rockland County's version of the symbolism of Ellis Island and the Statue of Liberty—the walk was appreciated for the freedom to talk and associate."

Arthur writes: "Many persons of the Jewish faith took the summer walk along the Boulevard, some just months away from the pogroms and ghetto poverty. Others were second-generation Americans, whose sense of family and ethnic history kept alive the stories and discrimination and the hope of a new nation offered."

The walkers reminded me of the Grand Concourse section in the Bronx where my family often went to visit my maternal grandmother's sister, who kept house and ran the office for a doctor in a large apartment across the street from the Grand Concourse Hotel. Walkers were in large numbers in that area, the women wearing their finest, and impressing me with the naturalness of their street outings. It was also from this apartment's rooftop that I got my first glimpse of Babe Ruth in the flesh rounding the bases at nearby Yankee Stadium (he was out of sight at his field position).

"As a young child," Arthur tells us, "riding my bike to the North Street School playground, I would see—and hear—the Boulevard walkers, women clad in fur wraps (you had to have something to show). Talking to friends and calling others on hotel porches along the way."

The Hillcrest-Spring Valley area was Arthur's bailiwick for several years, an area at that time known for its influx of summer vacationers. He tells us that Spring Valley in the vacation months would triple its population as "city dwellers escaped the heat and sought old friends in the best resort outside the Catskills."

As a newspaperman for more years than I care to mention, I was always on the lookout for a columnist who wrote mostly on local topics. They are invaluable to readers (and, of course, to circulation and the black side of the ledger). But too many of them move off the local peg and want punditry on national and world news. Arthur often gets his licks in on the issues of the world wider than the local stuff, but mostly he keeps the reader down the street or across the way in mind. And he keeps himself to one column a week, which, to my way of thinking, is enough because there are always editorials to write.

He has superb working habits, up and at 'em early in the morning. His roost is the office or tied to the home computer whenever an editorial is needed on some late-breaking local news. His language is neither pompous nor obscure, he writes for the reader who wants to know, who likes a historical note now and then, who has a deep interest in this triangle of not much land in southeastern New York state, who tells him about the cookie jar of suburban existence.

In the 2,600 essays Arthur Gunther has produced for his newspaper, there is always a sense of community and more than a scattering of expressive rainbows.

For many years we have been informed and enlightened by Art Gunther's editorials in The Journal News. We have also had the pleasure of reading his graceful and accomplished columns on Rockland's past and present. Art is a humane observer and a master storyteller with an insight for fresh detail. This collection of some of his work will give hours of enjoyment to discerning readers.

— Grant R. Jobson, Editorial Page Editor, The Journal News (retired).

Preface

These 100 columns represent a cross-section of the approximately 2,600 essays authored by me for The Journal News since 1981, under "The Column Rule" signature.

They include a look at the county's people, places and history, as well as general themes — short slices of life common to most Rocklanders, whether they were raised here or are later arrivals.

The collection is offered in response to public requests over the years and in a continuing effort by The Historical Society of Rockland County to chronicle the county in the defining century that was the 20th and is the early 21st.

Acknowledgement must be made of the many people mentioned in my columns. They, my wife, Lillian, and sons Arthur 4th and Andrew Edward, as well as their wives Laura and Patricia, respectively, have been and are the source of inspiration.

Torger Gram, my sixth-grade English teacher at the North Main Street School in Spring Valley, encouraged my love of writing, and I am grateful for that.

Rockland itself should be noted, for these pieces could not have been written without the county that has sustained my life.

Thanks to my various editors and proofreaders, including CynDee Royle and Holly Flieger of The Journal News and Albon Man and Jules Loh of The Historical Society of Rockland County. Special gratitude is extended to the Publications Committee of The Historical Society and to Thomas Casey, the society's president and Rockland County historian.

Finally, special thanks to: Xenia Kalinin, who processed and helped re-read these pieces; various Journal News staff, present and past, who encouraged the columns in the first place; and The Historical Society for publishing this work.

Arthur H. Gunther 3rd.

Section One
Rockland People

Nyack's other famous person

Nyack has its most famous resident in Helen Hayes, actress of stage and screen, and is home to other individuals of note, but the village also has a lady of special distinction who, while she is not known worldwide, is accorded respect, dignity and love.

Her name is Virginia Parkhurst, once a long-time reporter and women's editor for The Journal News. Now Nyack's official historian, she is a legend in her own right. She lives not too far from Helen Hayes, about four of Mrs. MacArthur's beloved rose gardens away, on Tallman Avenue. When she walks on Broadway toward Main, as Miss Hayes does, Virginia is apt to be stopped by just as many people wishing her a good day.

I saw Virginia Parkhurst last week, and we ended up walking some of Nyack's streets. I found I couldn't end most of my sentences because the conversation kept getting interrupted by "Hello, Miss Parkhurst, how are you?" or "What a nice day, Virginia, how good to see you." Many people caught her eye and her ear, as they have been doing since she began covering Rockland, and specifically Nyack, in 1934, two years after the Rockland County Evening Journal merged with the Nyack Daily News. (She had once been the editor of the News, and the day she was named to that post, the Evening Journal proclaimed in a headline: "News to be Edited by Girl.")

Virginia is one of those largely old-fashioned, seat-of-the-pants reporters who relied heavily on contacts and acquaintances to get the news on her "beat." Whether it was items for her "Magazine Page," which she both wrote and edited, or news of the maturing Nyacks, Virginia earned a reputation for endurance and thoroughness. Former village Mayor Al Volk has said that she "never left a meeting early and always gave both sides."

That fairness and completeness as a scribe have earned Virginia resident status as a knowledgeable, trustworthy Nyacker, a lady who has walked with the village through thick and thin and who long has had its best interest at heart.

As Volk has noted, "If you say 'Virginia' in Nyack, there is no doubt whom you're talking about."

Born in Hammonton, N.J., Virginia moved to Nyack in January 1929, after three years as a reporter for her hometown newspaper. Joining the staff of the Nyack Daily News, she remained with that newspaper until it merged with the Nyack Evening Journal in 1932 to become The Journal-News, at which time she left Nyack to work for the Englewood (N.J.) News and then the Oneonta (N.Y.) Star.

In 1934, she returned to Nyack and The Journal-News, where, except for a three-year stint with the Women's Army Corps during World War II, she remained until her retirement in 1974.

Did you catch that? "Three-year stint with the WACs." That's right. Virginia left Rockland and Nyack in the middle of a great war to seek great adventure. Maybe it was a mid-life sort of change, a new direction. Gosh knows she was entitled to that after an already noteworthy career in the newspaper business. Virginia came back safe and sound, though, with a renewed respect for Nyack and her profession. She was to cover many a Rockland meeting after that, to see numerous bylines on page one, to earn the further respect of readers.

Of course, Virginia Parkhurst did all that the first week on the job in Nyack. She's that sort of thorough journalist, and that's why people accord her regal dues on the streets of this village by the Hudson.

(December 19, 1989)

Definition of a Rocklander

We had a recent conversation with John A. Sutter, once and for a long time general manager and vice president of the Rockland Journal-News. He's a past Rocklander now, living in South Carolina and away from the people and themes that formed his very life. The question put to him in our short meeting was "Did he miss Rockland?"

"Yes," was the answer, but it was more than a quick, standard reply from a former countyite to a standard question put to anyone who moves on from a place. You might as well ask the same query of an Irishman late of Dublin or a Haitian who two years ago was residing in Port-au-Prince. The reply would have to be "yes," for it would be both bad form to say "no" and also a rejection of your background.

But Jack Sutter, true to his no-BS manner, gave more truth and substance to the reply than that. He really meant it. He likes South Carolina, though he may not adore it like South Carolinians. He's there because it is close to his daughter and is affordable and for other reasons.

But he would be driving up the lie detector needle if he did not say he missed a county where he went fishing with buddies as a child in Pearl River, where his parents instructed him in life and where, when he got up in the morning he heard the whistles of the steam trains rolling parallel to Main Street, or the sounds at the Dexter Co. plant that employed so many Pearl Riverites.

Jack could also not deny such friends as the well-informed, well-spoken, jack-of-all learning experiences that was his former New City neighbor, Col. (U.S. Army Ret.) Gerald Egelston. Nor could he forget the early days of covering Pearl River and other beats for The Journal-News, then rising in the ranks on the business and administrative sides to lead the newspaper through the suburban growth years after the Tappan Zee Bridge, the Palisades Interstate Parkway and the New York State Thruway came to be in the mid-'50s.

And to not admit that he misses so many of the people and days in his Rockland life, though Jack is not a misty-eyed sort who dwells on the past, would be to say that he once was a Rocklander but is not one now.

Every one of us came from somewhere, though we may live in Rockland now or have always. (I am a third-generation Rocklander myself.) We carry with us the traits and feelings and joys and, yes, sorrows of days past, wherever lived. That may be the grand shopping strip that was the Grand Concourse in the Bronx, or the fruit markets in Bensonhurst, Brooklyn, or the fields of Georgia or the plains of Iowa or the vacation seacoast of Ireland or the open markets of the Dominican Republic.

Each of us has memory of other times, other lives perhaps, that mark us as surely as we are marked now as Rocklanders. That holds true even for native countyites.

Jack Sutter recalls the Rockland of pre-World War II days, a quiet land of farms and fruit orchards where you knew just about everyone, where doors went unlocked, where neighbor tended to help neighbor, where parents were strict and schools, too. He is a product of those times and themes, just as you and I are products of our own times and themes (some, unfortunately, not always happy).

All this is to say that it is a mark of distinction to note you are a Rocklander, though that may be a different view and definition for you than it is for someone else. Surely a Rocklander of, say, 24 years in this county today is distinct from the Rocklander that was 24-year-old Jack Sutter of Pearl River decades ago. Any who live here, no matter how short the time, no matter how deeply or lightly they care about things Rockland, will be marked by our land, just as surely as anyone is anywhere, growing up in New Jersey or China.

Jack's heading back South soon, and he'll be a South Carolinian down there, but he will also be a Rocklander who could not shake off the dust of our many rocks if he tried. And neither can you.

I'd say that's a thing to be proud of and, for those who chose to do so, to wear as a campaign ribbon high on the chest.
(June 27, 1995)

Soldier's act of faith

Jerry Donnellan isn't the sort of person given to public emotional displays. He keeps a stiff upper lip, maybe because he learned to bite it as he lay seriously wounded in Vietnam.

Funny how all the soldiers who've seen their buddies die, who've tasted death, who can never get its stench out of their nostrils and dreams, never glorify war, never grandstand about patriotism and fulfilling one's duty.

Perhaps it's the high admission price to this select club, to this group of forever wounded soldiers, that makes them humble, that gives them an insight that is almost other-worldly.

And funny, too, how it is the quiet ones that we should heed the most, for they have much to say in both their reverence and irreverence. Jerry is one of those fellows. This veteran, who hawks for the causes of his fellow vets from Vietnam and other wars, recently sent me a package with a small note. It read, in just three words: "See, it worked."

The package contained a metal bracelet with the inscription, "Lt. Jeffrey N. Zaun, USN, 1-18-91, Iraq, POW/MIA." By now we all know that Lt. Zaun was shot down in the Persian Gulf war, captured, displayed on TV and made to criticize his country, and then imprisoned. We also know that the Cherry Hill, N.J., native has been freed and is now back home.

Donnellan wore the bracelet so that Zaun would not be forgotten. He performed a daily act of faith with his comrade of yet another war. He made no judgments about this or any other war. He simply wore a bracelet so that an airman would not be forgotten.

Many others did the same thing, civilians and ex-soldiers alike. And many Americans continue to wear bracelets for the POW/MIAs of other wars. Do you know that there are 389 missing Americans from the Korean War, which ended in 1953, *38 years ago*? There are also 2,283 Americans listed as missing in Southeast Asia.

These individuals have been forgotten by the United States through official convenience and bureaucratic oversight. Long ago, they were deemed expendable by Washington. But they are not forgotten, and it is people like Jerry Donnellan, people wearing bracelets, who keep hope alive that at least some of them will be rescued.

Donnellan is no more official Washington than he was official Army when he was wounded in 1969. He was just Joe Citizen hoping to survive and get home. When he lost a limb and redefined part of his soul in Vietnam, he made an unconscious, quiet pact with his buddies: To be with them forever, in spirit if not in physical reality.

His bracelets keep them alive.

(March 12, 1991)

A mayor of the people

John Balogh was a mayor/businessman who was happiest expounding on political themes. Forever fascinated by the democratic right of free speech, he always exercised it as if it were new to him. Perhaps he thirsted for it more than most because he spent the first 24 years of his life in turbulent Hungary.

This man of many opinions, this former mayor of Spring Valley who died Saturday one day short of his 85th birthday, said very little that wasn't expressed gracefully, with respect for the other person's views. He sensed others' democratic rights very well.

His court was Village Hall, of course, and the various (and ever more numerous) planning, zoning and regular village board meetings in that fantastic growth period from 1955 to 1965. His wisdom, decency and common sense brought a sense of direction to a village threatened by suburban change. If others who followed have not always gone the same way, it has not been for lack of the goal set by John Balogh.

Village Hall was the mayor's public stand, but his particular platform was the Majestic Barbershop at 46 Lawrence St. From 1930 until 1966, when it was torn down to make way for expansion of the old Ramapo Trust Co., this small ordinary haircutting shop was a meeting place of extraordinary dialogue. John Balogh, working at chair number one near the cash register and front window, would, between snips, offer opinions on FDR, the Depression, the war in Europe, the war in the Pacific, Truman, Eisenhower, the atom bomb, the cold war. Recollections of peasant uprising and European dictatorships would be mixed with commentary on the American right of dissent, the freedom of choice.

You did not have to sit in his chair to have a talk with him, for the mayor expounded at will, in every direction, in spontaneous oration that had heads nodding on men half-immersed in old magazines as they sat along the wall waiting their turn. Not all agreed with John Balogh, and he got as good as he gave, but almost to a man, his customers were his friends and came to his shop as much for the conversation as for the haircut.

9

That private forum, the Majestic Barbershop, eventually gave rise to the mayor's public stand at Village Hall. His views on Spring Valley's future, including the need to expand the commercial base, were well known, and the people who had listened to him so long saw the time was right to fulfill what seemed his destiny: to become mayor. And what fruitful terms they were, giving new life to a village increasingly in the long shadow of the new Tappan Zee Bridge.

After the mayor retired and the Majestic closed, Balogh was content with his flowers and fruit trees at his Washington Street home. He lived in the village 61 years and gave to it what seemed only proper: dedication, commitment, hope. In these times when people are constantly moving about, such deep, nurtured roots are a rarity. And that is too bad, since communities prosper best when people care enough to stay. The mayor stayed.

(September 25, 1984)

G. Jobson: Newspaperman

When you were a kid, maybe you walked in your father's shoes for fun. They were so big, and you did not think you would ever grow up enough to fill them.

Well, in an analogy extended to the work place, that's how I sometimes feel as editor of the Editorial Pages for the Rockland edition of The Journal News.

I have three principal predecessors who are my frame of reference here: Walter Williams, whose work goes back to the late 1920s and who was succeeded by Norman R. Baker in 1940 until 1970, and then Grant Jobson, who wrote editorials and managed the opinion pages from 1973 through 1986, also penning the well-received, deliciously irreverent column, "One Man's Rockland."

I could not offer the historical and factual background I do in my own daily work on these pages without understanding the opinions authored by Williams, Baker and Jobson. Though owners and publishers have changed in the years 1928-2005, and, of course, the newspaper's editorial stances ultimately reflect those sanctioned by the individual publisher, the threads of thought and community concerns in Rockland have been consistent in the past 75 or so years.

We have long called for orderly growth, for tolerance, for supporting education, for protecting Rockland's history, for political ethics, for recognition of this county's unique and important place in national history.

The continuation of such views, re-expressed as modern concern, has been the charge given me in this job since I took over the Edit Pages in January 1987, and I hope my eventual followers will also pick up the baton, which we all hold temporarily in a caretaking role.

Each day on these pages includes some writing, Monday through Sunday, here or at home. Same for my predecessors. Yet, despite the many thousands of words typed so far, I have never felt fully in the shoes of Williams, Baker and Jobson. I never knew Walter Williams, but he is a legend in the newspaper's history, having played a major role in making it a countywide sheet, dropping its name as the Nyack Evening Journal to become the Rockland County Evening Journal, and then The Journal News, after the merger with the old Nyack Daily News in 1932. He set the tone for key Rockland editorials on subjects still discussed today, and I reference those.

Norman Baker visited my eighth-grade journalism class at the old South Main Street School in Spring Valley in 1957, and little did I know I would someday sit in his seat here. His old editorials are plastered on my office walls, and I constantly reference his thorough work. I thank him for hiring me back in 1964.

Now to Grant Jobson, my full mentor, whose newsroom skills in copy editing and whose precise writing, infused with wit and brilliant twists of the language, were worthy of service on the old morning World of famous New York City newspaper fame.

Known as "Scoop Jobson" when he was a high school sports stringer in the late 1930s, Jobson would do 20 years on the Rockland County Times before coming to The Journal News in the early 1960s and then crafting a career as city editor, news editor, night editor and then Editorial Page editor.

I sit in his old office, where his rolled-up shirt sleeves, loose tie and yelps of near profanity over the doings of local politicos were as complete to the newsroom as our old General Electric office clock that has hummed for almost 50 years.

Jobson's office was old-fashioned newspaper. You could almost hear the teletype clacking, the Linotype casting lead slugs, the editor handing copy to the boy for typesetting.

Grant, who remains on this Earth today in New Hempstead, never knew how much he was respected here by the tribe nor how much he put down the well of institutional memory for edit writers like me.

I figure on my best day I half fill old Grant's shoes. Or Norman's. Or Walt Williams'.

Happy 84th birthday, Grantland Rice Jobson.
(October 21, 2005)

Have a seat on the couch...

The other day two guys hauled an old leather couch from The Journal-News building in West Nyack. They did so unceremoniously, with the red hulk ushered out like a dismissed worker.

It deserved a better fate. If the couch could talk, not only would the couch be red, for those who sat on it were sometimes flushed in anger, sometimes in embarrassment and regret. Others would be gleeful.

A little history about the couch: Straight out of the 1930s, it was by the 1980s a luxurious half-couch with leather deeply polished by many workers' posteriors. It was the sort you used to find in lawyers' offices (never in doctors' offices, though – why?). For many years it was in the general manager's office, a no-nonsense place on the top floor at 53 Hudson Ave. in the old Journal News building in downtown Nyack. This was the room where you got a raise, were chewed out or shown the door. In all three cases, you sat on the red leather couch. Occasionally, you received a compliment or got a promotion while seated there.

I brushed past the couch – nervously – when I was hired by the late Norman R. Baker as a copy boy in the early 1960s. I sat on it with former Journal-News photographer Andrew Dickerman after we had been kicked around while on assignment during a police raid on a bar in West Nyack. We had been attacked by the owners, and Jack Sutter, the Journal-News general manager, wanted all the details. Jack was always fair with you – he listened quietly but he also wanted both sides to every story. You sweated under his entirely appropriate grilling – sweated on the red leather couch.

When this newspaper added a Sunday edition in March 1972, the couch got a real workout. There were many meetings in the GM's office, and the leather never got cold. Orders flew back and forth in that room amid excitement approached only by the doubling of the old Journal-News building some years before.

When the newspaper moved to its present West Nyack location in April 1982, the red leather couch went with us. This time it was consigned to a conference room, where it served editors like me who preferred to slump rather than sit on hard, plastic chairs. It was also used by Grant Jobson, my predecessor as editorial page editor, as a place to take a nap.

Grant's work hours were like his general approach to life – do the work as needed, not by the time clock. You put in the effort required, no matter how long it took. And if you could, you worked when the creative juices were flowing best. Sometimes that was 2 in the morning. At 4 a.m. Grant might hit the couch for a few winks.

I don't know who designed the couch, but he/she was brilliant. It was soft and inviting, particularly if you had been hunched over a desk for hours while seated in a hard chair. Once tempted – and as beckoned by the GM – you plopped down in comfort. This set you up for the chew-out, which was usually deserved. The deepness of the couch also made you sit lower than the boss, which must have been intentional. It also was difficult for you to get up once your talk was over. No graceful exit, just an awkward one, which underscored your insignificance and which put the fear of whatever in you once again.

Believe it or not, that led to some good newspapering days.

The couch is gone now, but at least I managed to get a glimpse of it while it was being carted out. I didn't get to drink a toast to it, though, or to its many occupants, to Jack Sutter or the other GMs who glared at it and all of us from on high.

I don't know what its fate is, where it will now reside or who will sit in it. I won't get another chance to sit on the couch in fear, anticipation or even in happiness. (I also won't get to look for change under its cushions anymore.)

A new couch may take its place, but I'm not sure it will be as deceptively inviting as the old one. Whether that proves positive is one the jury will be out on for a long time.

(October 24, 1987)

Rabbi's Christmas visit

The funeral of Rabbi Josef Soloveitchik on Wednesday in Monsey brought many mourners and much due respect for a man who helped pave the way for the Orthodox Jewish community in Spring Valley. His life was recalled in glowing terms, as deserved, but missing was an anecdote that perhaps tells more about the rabbi than anything else.

It is a story of a younger, smaller Spring Valley. A tale of a summer bungalow community that did not lose its Jewish flavor once September had arrived and the long winter had set in. Most of all, it is an anecdote of understanding and, therefore, of hope.

Rabbi Soloveitchik came to Spring Valley in 1932, the same year my grandparents and their son, my father, moved into an apartment between Madison Avenue and Main Street. The rabbi would form the Congregation Sons of Israel, a mainstream Orthodox congregation that he headed for many years. His congregants came mainly from the "hill" section of the village, where many of the summer bungalows and resort hotels were located.

In those days, actually until the early '60s, living and growing up in Spring Valley meant being acquainted with Jewish traditions, the Yiddish language and, perhaps most important, a philosophical way of life, a way of looking at and accepting the ups and downs that we all get hit with.

It did not matter that you were not Jewish. Gentile or otherwise, you caught the flavor, you understood the language, you appreciated the philosophy. Like the air you breathe and the food you eat, the environment had an effect on you and your thinking.

The Soloveitchik anecdote was born of such an environment. In the '30s, deep in the Depression that sobered this land and its people, on a cold winter night, Christians gathered to celebrate the birth of Jesus Christ in a Midnight Mass at the old St. Joseph's Church on Main Street in Spring Valley.

Attending were John Romaine, a native who operated Ro-Field's Appliance store near the corner of Main and Church streets. Romaine was a village fixture, a bright, smiling man who was known to most everyone in this small community of under 5,000 people. He had friends everywhere and his soft-spoken, undemanding way of talking – and listening – was a magnet. One of those attracted to him was Rabbi Soloveitchik.

15

On this cold night, when those of one religion were celebrating an inner warmth, the good rabbi accompanied a good resident to Mass. I was not there, but the account told me years later by John Romaine had the rabbi attending in respect, not participating but part of the larger community nevertheless.

This was the way it was in the Spring Valley I knew as a boy. Gentiles picked up Jewish ways and Jews found something in common with Gentiles. Rabbi Soloveitchik made no judgments about a religion he did not accept, and John Romaine did not bring the rabbi to Mass for the purposes of conversion.

They were just two human beings who had long ago surrounded themselves in the friendship of mutual respect and who were on this particular night observing a Christian custom. The next day, they might be at a synagogue or deep in a discussion about Jewish philosophy.

Such was the character of Rabbi Josef Soloveitchik and John Romaine. Now they are both gone and, I am sure, friends once again.

(May 23, 1987)

Gus Weltie and The Indian

If you drive up the small, twisting road leading to the High Tor Vineyards in New City, to the woods that lie at the rear feet of High Tor and Little Tor, you may see the ghost of "The Indian" in Maxwell Anderson's play "High Tor."

The Indian represented the red man's ancestors in this famous 1930s play. He was The Land. He was the soul of" High Tor." He was what the trap rock people would try to destroy if they took the mountain and pounded its glacial rock into wallboard. The Tor was saved, of course, but The Indian also did not win in the human sense. His days were numbered when the play began, for his kind and their ways were already misplaced in modern society.

In the end, The Indian died and was buried with his ancestors' spirits on the Tor. In death, The Indian forever claimed the mountain as he could not do in life.

I'm reminded of The Indian by an old newspaper piece that Bill Koerner, a reader from Haverstraw, recently sent me. It's about another old High Tor hand, Gus Weltie, who worked below the Tor for many years. It's a story worth repeating.

In 1894, Gus came to work for High Tor Farm and Elmer Van Orden, supposedly for just a few days. Gus had been brought up in an orphanage and sent to work on an Ulster County farm, but he found it too remote and ran away. Finally, he drifted to Haverstraw and began working for John Wilkes, who ran a milk route.

Then Gus heard Elmer wanted someone to work on the farm, and he went over to High Tor. He worked there for 48 years and was paid $5 a month, never getting a raise. He never took a vacation and never traveled farther than New York City (maybe once or twice there).

Gus and Elmer worked two farms and a milk route, getting up at 2 a.m. to collect milk from neighboring farms. Then, as now, High Tor cast its shadow over the land, but Gus had little time to think aloud about its magnificence and beauty.

When Elmer died in 1942, he left much of his property to Gus, a nephew and a niece. In the years that followed his long working sojourn on the Tor, Gus, a quiet man, made no speeches about the mountain, but he was a passionate fighter for its protection.

Like The Indian, Gus Weltie articulated his feelings about his beloved mountain inwardly, adding to the depth of his soul and, ultimately, High Tor's. His actions spoke for him: He remained near the mountain just as The Indian would not leave.

In a modern world, where roots and their nourishment are hard to come by, the stories of Gus Weltie and The Indian prove an anchor to what really matters.

(February 28, 1987)

Accomplished, with dignity

Take a concerned person in his/her 30s, give the individual a cause, and you've lit a fire that can consume obstacles and make the world a better place. What about an older person, though? Isn't age 83 a retiring time? Aren't you supposed to be gracing the rocking chair and letting the battles be fought by the young blokes?

Not if you're Isabelle Savell. This wonderfully calm, articulate, super-bright lady and defender of the environment spent her entire life working hard for improvement, either self-betterment or to help others. She died Thursday after a bout with cancer and, while that assault dragged Isabelle away from us, never once did she let its punches knock her from her self-appointed rounds.

I met Isabelle through this page. Occasionally, she would write letters about the need to protect the beauty and ecology of the Hudson River or Grand View, where she lived for decades, or about plans for a second Tappan Zee Bridge. More often, she would send me missives and packets of information on who was doing what about traffic plans and river clean-up.

In this business, you attract such sources, but most of them have a particular ax to grind and they lobby you to death. Isabelle never did this, preferring to act as the reporter and editor she once was and simply assemble the facts so that others could take up the story and present a fair view of things. This she did without anger, without foot-stomping, but with grace. I am certain that even her opponents bowed to Isabelle's dignity.

She and I shared more than a journalistic background. Isabelle was once editor of the Nyack Evening Journal, the forerunner of this newspaper. She worked in what is now a Chinese laundry on South Broadway in Nyack, a stone's throw from 53 Hudson Avenue, where for a long time I pounded keys and did many other things until The Journal News moved to West Nyack. Isabelle's duties included sweeping the floor, firing up a pot-bellied office stove and helping make up pages in hot metal.

It was an ink-stained profession and a craft that knew long hours and much detail. There was built-in humility – sweeping floors and getting chewed out by readers – and the time and place and events served to test Isabelle's mettle and cast her determination.

The last years of her life were devoted to the Tappan Zee Preservation Coalition, which has been fighting for protection of the Hudson River shore. A primary goal has been to have Rockland's Tappan Zee section designated a "scenic area" so as to make a new bridge and other river development more difficult to accomplish.

Isabelle realized, as have others, that the Thruway and Palisades Interstate Parkway have sliced Rockland into quarters, taking away valuable and beautiful green space and giving us noise and pollution in their stead. She recalled when South Nyack's downtown was wiped out by the bridge approach and shuddered when she thought what would happen if another crossing were built to accommodate interstate travelers who merely pass through Rockland and benefit none of us.

On Thursday at her Grand View home, a letter was brought to Isabelle, a letter indicating that the state had indeed designated the shore as a scenic area. News of that great victory was being read to her as she slipped away, and the feeling is she took the information with her as she left this void, passing over the great Tappan Zee and marveling at the God-given beauty humankind can protect when it has a conscience to do so.
(November 1, 1988)

Memorial Park, with George

Why it is I'm not sure, but the sun seems larger and brighter when you're young. Maybe it's because you notice it more from the leisure of a swing, a merry-go-round or a walk to school. Riding in a car to work or on some errand, busy with this or that, doesn't allow much time for smelling the flowers.

I can recall a few spectacular views of the sun, including some in Spring Valley's Memorial Park, where my father would drop my brother Craig and me off so he could do some early-day shopping. This was about 1950, shortly after the park had opened – it had been the village dump for many years – and a large expanse of green lawn, a gleaming white war monument, a lake with rented rowboats and a children's playground now covered the spot. It was a quiet, safe, really quite beautiful park – a tribute to the people, politicians and businessmen who sought to renew the Valley after World War II.

My brother and I had a habit in those days whenever we visited the park. We would go up to one of the candy stores on Main Street and get some soap bubbles to play with as we sat on the swings. They cost 5 cents a bottle, and while that meant going without candy, somehow it seemed traditional and, therefore, worth it.

The rest of our playtime was on the cheap. We stayed away from the water because we were told to. We went as high as we could on the swings, kicking our feet back and forth to gain so much speed that we thought the metal mooring poles would come loose. Most of all, we liked the merry-go-round, which is still there. Craig would get on the device and have me give it a push and then jump on (he usually got me to do the work), my body swaying outward like a full-blown sail as gravity resisted my movements.

The merry-go-round was a mecca for all the kids about, including George D'Loughy, a friend who lived in Nanuet but whose father helped run one of the markets in Spring Valley. More often than not, his father would send him down the hill to the park to keep him out of trouble, and old George would join my brother on the merry-go-round, giving me two people to push. That was OK, because George and Craig were (and are) good guys. They'd end up doing something together and, if I wasn't joining them, I'd have another opportunity simply to sit down and look about, maybe notice the sun.

In later years, George and I touched base in school and here and there afterward, but I usually remember him from the few times we met on the merry-go-round because those were beginning days for all of us. The sun was at its brightest, or so it seemed, and while I didn't make a particular effort to watch it, you notice so much when you're age 7 that such simple things like the sun make a lasting impression. It's the sort of daylight that you carry with you always, especially for the darker moments.
(July 11, 1989)

Tale of a hardware man

You look at the box of wood screws and read the printed words, which don't mean much: "Slotted 1-inch flat head steel wood screws, bright zinc chromate, 100 count." You find this sort of reading on any hardware container.

What you don't find all that often is a hand-written note that the screws were purchased, in this case, on May 7, 1982, and that the entire box cost $1.90. George W. Hadeler Jr. wrote that added info when I picked up the screws at his Pearl River hardware store, accompanied by the verbal extra that I would probably have the screws so long that many years later I would look at the box and marvel at both the date and the price.

That was the sort of homespun, customer-interested touch George Hadeler gave to his work at the store his father, George W. Sr., began in 1905. Hadeler died last week at 86, a good, long life, for sure, and one that touched many a person in numerous generations.

He was a fixture at the hardware store, selling this or that, little do-dads and whatchamacallits that have been keeping the American homestead together since the wagons began to roll westward. No town is really a town without a hardware store and, while the chains have pushed aside too many of them, Rockland still has a number of which it can be proud. George Hadeler ran one, as his sons, George III and Paul, do now.

He would be the first to tell you that he simply operated a store, a good store. He was a hardware man, one of those multi-knowledgeable people who have to have on mental tap a little bit about everything for the home and yard. Hardware men are as sought after for their advice as for their wares, and George was one of them.

He was also part of American lore. Jimmy Stewart didn't stay in Indiana because he was called elsewhere by thespian voices, but he admits to a twinge of nostalgia now and then for the life of his father, who was a hardware man. Many a person, under stress and belittled, bothered and bewildered by life in general, has wanted to "go off somewhere and buy a hardware store."

There may or may not be calm in such resolution, but it's a good thing there are hardware men (and women) in the world, for without them Saturday mornings would be a bit more dull, the faucets would drip because we would buy the wrong size washers, and we'd come home with more bolts than we needed.

George W. Hadeler Jr. was a hardware man, and that's all his epitaph has to read.

(April 11, 1989)

Rocco Fazio, lifelong teacher

You never outgrow the need to have a teacher, a mentor, to correct you. I learned that the other night from Rocco Fazio, who was head teacher at the North Main Street School in Spring Valley when I was attending it during the early to mid-1950s.

Mr. Fazio and I met at a gathering of other Spring Valleyites – present and former – and he reminded me that he never was the principal or teaching principal at North Main. In an earlier column, I gave him such a promotion. Actually, Keith Apgar was principal of both the North and South Main Street schools. Mr. Fazio taught social studies, had a homeroom and also was *head teacher*. I guess the fact that I was in the office often enough and that he was frequently there, too, confused my memory and made me think of him as a teaching principal. He certainly had the presence of one.

Now, it was not a major gaffe to give Mr. Fazio an incorrect title, but I bring it up to make a point, actually two points: As much as I write – two columns a week for almost 10 years now and numerous editorials – I am no oracle, no source of undisputed information. I am sometimes full of hot air, and I don't mind it too much if you burst the balloon once in a while.

I have the advantage of having lived and/or worked in Rockland virtually all my life and I have a decent memory. I also have an interest in things past, so I have catalogued many incidents, names, etc., in my brain. I frequently pull one out and build an anecdotal piece around it, but either because my memory plays tricks or I take limited license to enhance the dramatics, the facts may be a bit rearranged. (I usually try to be accurate, though.)

Working in my favor is the fact that not everyone else shared the same history or interest, so I can be a generalist and get away with it. I'm boosted because rarely do two people recall the same incident in exactly the same way, probably since we all take from any moment according to our needs.

The second point: It's good for the soul to be reminded that you don't stand on a pedestal, that you make mistakes – sometimes lots – and that it's in the interests of accuracy and credibility when you get a mild comeuppance.

I never had Rocco Fazio for social studies, although he did instruct me in behavior, and I was in his electricity club when he was at the newly formed Spring Valley Junior High School. As I recall, he was friendly with the students, including me, and tried to give them a boost when they needed it. That means he was my teacher, too, even if I did not have him for a subject.

Apparently, he's still my teacher. Good.
(October 30, 1990)

Henry Kulle, 'Tire King'

When I was a 16-year-old, first-time driver in Spring Valley, there was no name more important to me than Henry Kulle.

This fine fellow ran a still-famous tire business in an equally famous alleyway between Lawrence and Main streets. If you had a jalopy, as I did (1950 Chevrolet, bought from Drotch Motors in West Nyack for $150), you visited Kulle sooner or later.

Probably sooner. The four-ply tires of those days (no radials) didn't last long and, with king pins and other suspension parts a bit loose on an old car, the tires could need replacement at less than 5,000 miles.

My first visit to Henry Kulle, Inc., was an experience never to be forgotten. Unlike other tire shops where you might wait in a warm room while someone changed your tires, it was all outside at Kulle's.

You got in line in the alley, entering from Lawrence Street. Then you stood in the alley while Henry and the Ball family came over to your car, sized up your needs and disappeared into really old buildings to dig out your tires.

They always had what you needed, and amazing Henry knew exactly where everything was stored. I believe that if you had come in with a 1924 Chevy, he would have had the right tire, retrieved after a few seconds.

The 28 Main St. shop marked 100 years in 1996, with business beginning as a harness and saddle repair store run by Edward, Henry's father. Cars have been lining up on Lawrence since the 1920s, with the scene immortalized in a painting by artist Robert Burghardt of Stony Point.

In the early 1920s, Henry Kulle started making convertible touring tops for the open cars of the day, and then began dealing in tires and car batteries. (He had struck a deal with the old Widmann's Bakery behind his buildings that their delivery trucks would start each morning in return for battery and tire purchases.)

Henry Kulle never sat down on the job. A thin, healthy man who ate a banana every day and walked for exercise, he literally rushed from customer to customer, offering quiet advice in fast-paced talk, his eyes darting to the ground often, as he could be a shy man.

He loved people and his customers, serving numerous generations of the same family. He also gave young people advice, such as how to keep a car running well, and the importance of hard work.

His Saturday morning lines, in particular, were like the old country stores, or barbershops, where men gathered to talk about politics. Henry always had a word or two on that subject.

Or he could offer a ribald joke. He had quite a repertoire. Known around the village as the "Tire King," Henry Kulle continued to work until his death in 1987 at age 84. The shop is now run by relatives Jim and Tom Ball, with the Kulle traditions continuing.
(July 17, 2001).

Bill Koerner added to life

You get all kinds of phone calls from all manner of people in my business as a newspaper columnist and Editorial Page editor, and you learn to anticipate each one with curiosity but also skepticism. So many people have their own agendas and think maybe the newspaper could be a conduit to success. No complaints, though – the calls come with the job, and sometimes I can help.

Every once in a while there is a refreshing break in this routine, when I receive a call or a letter from someone who greatly adds to the pleasures of being a lifelong Rocklander in the Rockland-oriented job of local newspapering.

About five years back, the phone rang and I picked it up to hear the voice of a fellow from Haverstraw who, I realized after I later saw him, was the spitting image of Henry Travers, the great '30s character actor who played Clarence the angel in "It's a Wonderful Life."

That comparison had added depth. Bill Koerner was about as kindly and interested in human folk as was Clarence.

It made him boiling mad to see government wasting money or not doing the people's job. He had been a worker for the state Department of Transportation and recalled days when no pothole went unfilled and no guardrail was left loose just because there were budget cuts. (In fact, last year he took the state to task for a dangerous guardrail off Route 9W just above his Dutchtown home.)

He also fought a local quarry when it changed its operations and kept him awake at night. But most of all, Bill, a lifelong Haverstraw resident, was a history buff, meticulously clipping old articles from the Haverstraw Times and other papers, having them photocopied and then pasting the clippings in bound volumes, which he would give to his friends.

Former Editorial Page Editor Grant Jobson and I have a whole bunch, on subjects ranging from early 20th century days in Rockland to World War II events to post-war growth. They are handsomely done and, when I get a breather in later life from this everyday toil, I will be sure to pore over them fully.

From time to time, Bill, who took years to call me Arthur rather than Mr. Gunther (I figure that only my father can be called that), would phone me at home or at work, always with an idea for a column or a photograph or an editorial. His voice would always be reassuring and positive and his comments downright interesting.

About three weeks ago, I received my last call from Bill, on a Sunday. He wanted to let me know that he had left a new book of clippings with a friend at work. (It was on Rocklanders in military service during World War II). We had a short chat about the Hudson River, which he loved, and other things about the county, and we both then said goodbye and moved on to the other events of the day.

Our phone goodbyes were the last ones between us. Bill Koerner died July 29 at his home at the age of 71.

His spirit lives, however, for we are all changed by every good person that we meet. I will long recall his outlook on Rockland's uniqueness, his love of history, his decency, his concern for me in particular. I'm glad – I'm honored – that he called me years back.

Bill Koerner added a dimension to my life and my work, and that's a legacy that will continue until I, too, am no longer here.

And I like to think that I will also pass along some of my own concerns, and in that way I will continue Bill's as well.

We are all part and parcel of everyone else.

(August 11, 1992)

Unsung who ensure stability

I was at the Nyack Street Fair on Sunday, immersed in that sea of humanity bent on perusing, eating and otherwise having a good time. I was struck by the size of the crowd and realized that each of these many people was an individual, a person with feelings, accomplishments and a record of living.

That got me to thinking about unsung people, those hard-working types who don't make newspaper headlines but who consistently achieve and who because of their daily reliability support the world. There are many such people and we will never know their names. Their effect and importance are like the inner workings of a fine clock. The clock runs well for years, and we never look inside to observe the properly functioning parts. We simply take the net effect – the accurate keeping of time – for granted.

I'll give you an example. Martha (Marty) Erickson, a reader and original Rocklander, sent us a letter about a number of things and included a newspaper clipping from the old Rockland Leader, a great weekly out of Spring Valley. The Jan. 2, 1964, piece detailed a man named Clarence E. (Pete) Erickson, Marty's father-in-law.

Now, most county residents never heard of Pete, yet he has been such a solid citizen that it's fair to say he has been for many years one of the finer inner workings of the clock that helped Rockland keep up with the times.

Pete, who is now 88, was born in the Brick Church section of Ramapo and went through Spring Valley schools. His uncle had a milk business, and Pete eventually made a deal with him to distribute the milk. This he did for many years, operating the Woodside Dairy. He would stop off at many businesses in the county, including the old Plaza Restaurant in Spring Valley where a young boy named Eugene Levy (later to be our state senator) worked with his father.

Pete plied his trade for 35 years or so, taking no vacations, and as the Leader article reported, "making no pretensions about being a big businessman." He had a ready smile, sincere drawl and much charm. He became known all over because of his milk route and the community service that grew from it – church work, trustee of School District No. 8, trustee of the Rockland County Vocational and Guidance Board, president of the state Association of Vocational Education and Extension Boards, master of Athelstane Lodge, F. & A.M. and for more than 20 years a Ramapo town councilman.

Last year Levy presented Pete with a special Masonic award, and the senator said he owed much to Pete because Erickson helped Levy develop his sense of service, integrity, honor and politics.

Obviously, Pete Erickson did more than that – he influenced scores of people, "all, mind you," as the Leader noted, "without being pushy or posing as a do-gooder."

He was another largely unsung citizen who kept the foundation from caving in.

Thank goodness we have them.

(July 24, 1990)

'Butch Logue' understood

The facts are these: John "Butch" Logue of Nyack lived 95 years and some months. He worked in the printing trade and at this newspaper until he was 80. He resided in Nyack for 89 seasons. He was a World War I Marine. He was a 75-year member of Mazzeppa Engine Co. No. 2, and he was a dedicated, through-and-through Rocklander who demanded respect for his community.

But Butch was also something else: He was tied to generations long forgotten. He was, by virtue of his age and experience, the wise manwho walked among us. He would regale patrons at O'Donoghue's in Nyack with tales of the first airplanes landing in Upper Nyack in the 1920s, Nyack as a resort area in the early part of this century and traveling across the Hudson to Tarrytown by sleigh when the river froze over.

He knew the days when electricity was supplied for just hours daily and when most people still had gas lamps. He drove Mazzeppa's first motorized fire truck. He recalled Nyack in the tougher days of the Depression and in the late '50s and early '60s when strip-shopping lured customers away from Main Street and Broadway. He also saw urban renewal and the antique shops resurrect the village, and he would often spend warm Sunday afternoons sitting on the steps of Marine Midland Bank, watching visitors and giving them a sharp retort if they littered or let dogs dirty the sidewalks.

Butch Logue was also a printer of the old school, who learned his craft in that almost-dead art of printing sticks, Linotypes, handset type, Ludlow casting machines and precision. He was his own boss for 44 years at the Ethlas Press Co. in Nyack and then came to what was then The Journal-News in 1965. Actually, it was a return since he had worked for the Nyack Evening Journal, a predecessor of this newspaper, before the Great War.

Kind and quick to give a shy smile, Butch was a good man. He was married to the same woman, Mae, for 49 years until she passed away in 1970, leaving a major hole in his life that years of wandering Nyack only partially filled.

This man did not mean to become a fixture in the village. He did not intend to become popular, to be honored by parades and newspaper stories. It's just that he outlived so many other people, and took to walking the town, visiting his friends at the firehouse and tavern daily and speaking to people on the street.

In this fashion, and because of the depth and breadth of ordinary experience, Butch became a man who had "been there before." He understood people so well because he had been a person himself for so long. He had seen it all.

Such a person becomes a vital part of the backdrop that is the very fabric of life.

That's why he'll be missed, even though Nyack had the pleasure of his company (and vice versa) for almost nine decades.
(July 28, 1992)

Carl Booth: Defining moment

Youth has its defining moments, those flashes of light that open doors of understanding which will probably not close in your lifetime. As you age, you may recall the actual event or you may not; that is of little importance; what counts is that once there was such a moment or two.

One arrived for me in the fifth grade. The scene was the gym at the North Main Street School, Spring Valley, in 1954. We had just gotten a new coach, who took a military approach to athletics. We had to line up, bodies straight, an elbow length away from the fellow next to us and yell "present!" when Coach DePasquale called the roll.

He also did not tolerate talking, and his favorite punishment for violators like me, an inveterate day dreamer and occasional talker, was to "go to the mat," which meant wrestling some other poor Joe who also ignored the rules.

One day, when I got the treatment, I went to the mat with Carl Booth, a fellow who lived with his mason father on Twin Avenue. In fact, the family resided in the house that the father built, and his great craftsmanship is still to be seen on that home, now in other hands.

The Booth family was as important to the Spring Valley area as the DeBauns or the Sherwoods or the Talmans, for these were solid families with long roots and service to the community.

The Booth family was also black, a fact that usually turned no heads in the Spring Valley of my youth in the 1940s and '50s.

But I had my unreasonable fears, even at age 10-11, and when the coach ordered me to the mat with Carl Booth, I wondered with some fear what it would be like to fight him. I had wrestled with my brother, who is as white as I am. I had fooled around with friends in water fights, etc., but they were all white. I had never wrestled a black kid.

Well, I went to the mat and took my medicine, jumping all over Carl but trying to be gentle because I just wasn't the punching sort of fellow (probably because I was too chicken). I thought for a moment that Carl would knock me silly in my weakness, maybe because he was black. I mean, prejudice says there's extra power there, right?

You know what, though? Carl Booth, as quiet and shy a person as I was, was just as afraid of fighting this white boy as I was of jumping all over him. He, too, faked the scene and made it look like we were really wrestling hard. He, too, did not want to go the mat, to be forced into a situation that for us, at least at the moment, had no meaning.

I don't think the good coach paired us on the mat as a black/white thing. He did not seem to care about color. He just wanted quiet and attention in his gym. But I'm glad he did. Not because of the intended lesson. I'm sure I talked in gym after that day, and so did Carl. I'm not certain the discipline lesson ever took hold on either of us.

And, no, there wasn't a turning point in race relations for either Carl or me. Neither of us had a bent in any extreme before or after the mat event. (Folks in the Valley of my day were largely like that, a bunch of not-rich folks just getting on with life.)

What the mat did teach Carl and me, though, was to overcome unreasonable fears. In the minute or two I had to think about fighting Carl and his fighting me, we surely suffered more than during the wrestling. I know I exaggerated what would happen. And when I found out that black Carl was just like me and that white Art was just like him, we suddenly were just two 10-year-old goof-offs.

A defining moment.

(July 26, 1994)

John Marsilio and the Hi-Ho

There isn't a newspaperman or woman around who hasn't ambled up to the rail that is our sometime confessional. For imbibers and not, a particular tavern or two has often been the journalist's occasional home away from home, the office apart from the office. It is where non-deadline dreams that may never be are explored, where boasts that were never fulfilled are made, where for the moment there is no Big Brother and where general society has no admission.

The soul of a newspaper may be in its flat-footed, shoes-worn, hardened-to-the-grit reporters, and that soul may emote at the computer terminal to the printed page, but it is in the off-time, in the confessional, that the newspaperman's very being is given the shower that it needs to stay fresh.

That cleansing could be a drink (thankfully less so today because even journalists realize the dangers of too much alcohol). It could be conversation with a fellow or gal in the profession. Or relief simply could come from staring into space.

It's the *environment* that counts, the place that allows you to let it all hang out. You have to be among your kind to successfully vent the pent-up gas in any profession, for there is subtle and unstated but obvious understanding in like company.

For years Nyack village had a particular place where we newspaper people could shake off the nails from our souls. It was called the Hi-Ho, and the fact that it was once a speakeasy made it all the more trustworthy. For decades, it was a fixture off Main Street, and my colleagues, particularly my predecessors like former Editorial Page Editor Grant Jobson, stopped by regularly.

They would not have done so, I suspect, if the Hi-Ho hadn't made us feel welcome. Newspaper people are sometimes like cats – they sense the territory. If it isn't friendly, they move on, no backward glance given. The Hi-Ho never gave us cause to do that, and it frequently provided us with nine lives' worth of soulful rejuvenation.

That was possible because of John E. Marsilio, for 30 years the owner of the Hi-Ho. John and his brother George, who later ran the Hi-Ho until it was sold and reopened as Chelsea-on-Hudson, liked journalists.

All journalists, whether we came from this newspaper or the Daily News, the Herald-Tribune, the World Telegram & Sun or any of the many other metropolitan papers whose journalists lived in Rockland.

Both Marsilios knew your drinks, knew when to talk to you, when to back off. They understood that we cats sometimes want company and sometimes do not, that we can walk in on a tight wire and that we have to loosen the tension before we come down.

John Marsilio died Thursday at 74 in a veterans hospital in Beacon. The place is close to the Hudson River that was his backyard for most of his life, so at least he may have felt a bit at home. Perhaps his last thought included some stills of his many days and nights at the Hi-Ho, when a good bartender and host knew that the stew doesn't cook if the pot is watched.

All we ever wanted at the Hi-Ho was to unwind and dream of other moments, realized and unrealized. John and George always gave us that.

Here's one for you, fellows.

(May 14, 1991)

Herb, Pearl River's 'mayor'

Every community in Rockland has an unofficial "mayor," the person who most defines the community, its past, its soul, its very being.

For a long time now, Pearl River has been fortunate to have Herbert Peckman, a liquor store owner, former state Senate postmaster and hamlet historian.

Herb is celebrating his 90th birthday Thursday, so it is time to write about this hale, hearty and most-interesting "young" man.

Five years ago, the then 85-year-old raconteur and Pearl River activist authored a book, "Pearl River Then and Now," a unique perspective on the town where he was born and raised.

Nancy Cacioppo of The Journal News, in a feature article, wrote that "The 37-page memoir, illustrated with vintage photographs, is more than the history of his hometown. It captures the flavor of small-town America that has faded from the national scene."

As Herb then noted, the focus in his Pearl River youth was on the family, with everyone doing his share. There were gardens; preserves were put up; there was constant house cleaning from the dust of the roads; there were coal and wood to be brought in and fires to be banked at night for heating in the early morning.

People worked six days a week and 10-hour days. A man's word was his bond, and local tradesmen were counted on for durable goods and on-time delivery.

In all this there was a sense of community, and Herb has been chasing that rainbow ever since he first saw it and enjoyed its comfort as a child in this "Town of Friendly People."

Now very much an enclave of those with Irish roots, Pearl River once had mostly families of German heritage, and the sense of industriousness and order was as important then as family is now to the Irish Americans. Each group has imparted special flavor to this hamlet.

Herb has said that the average yearly family income of his era was $1,213, "but the average cost of a new home was only $3,395, and you could buy a brand new Ford car right off the showroom floor for $780 ... and drive it on gas that only cost 10 cents a gallon."

When he grew up and set himself to the task of building his own family, Herb bought a Dutch colonial-style home from a customer whose "niece was Gene Tierney, a beautiful movie actress who starred in many hits, and she frequently spent her weekends at the house."

The year Herb was born, 1911, there were perhaps just 1,000 people in Pearl River. Today, there are about 22,000. "You used to know everybody and everything about the whole town. I used to do election canvassing and knew how many people lived in every house. But people don't stay put any more," he has lamented.

Herb's health and longevity are surely traced to good genes and healthy habits but also to his motto that "a busy man is a happy man."

Peckman's Liquors, the family business that he founded decades ago, is now run by his son, Donald. Before that he was postmaster of the New York state Senate for three years in the 1930s. Herb has also been chairman of the Pearl River Democratic Party and president of the hamlet Rotary Club.

Happy Birthday to Herbert Peckman, who continues to write us letters about Pearl River's fine past and the absolute need for a sense of community in a hurried world.

Perhaps we should honor his day by following one of Herb's maxims: "Wear out, don't rust out."

(August 14, 2001)

Harry's in the blocks

The very day that famed Rockland track star Harry Jackson passed away, the U.S. Olympic Track and Field Trials for this sport began in Sacramento. Given the great spirit that inhabits this world from beyond, it is certain that he was there, too, in the starting blocks.

Actually, Harry who was 85 when he left us Friday at Good Samaritan Hospital in Suffern, was always in the starting blocks. This Spring Valleyite and longtime Hillcrest resident literally leapt from his bed almost every day of his life.

You saw Harry Jackson running everywhere, whether it was mowing a lawn (his big strides got him across any expanse in seconds); delivering milk for the Erickson dairy before school; or digging a grave by hand so neatly that it was the work of art he intended it to be for those who had departed.

Now Harry himself is gone, to be buried today from the same Brick Church and in the same next-door cemetery where he spent so many decades of his life.

Whenever Harry Jackson or his sons, Harry Jr. and Gene, or his grandsons dug a grave there or at other cemeteries, including the two county veterans graveyards, Harry was sure to look about and silently say hello to the many neighbors and friends he had made sure would get a neat and respectable final resting place.

This man was a truly decent sort, the kind of well-respected Rocklander who built this county, whose word was better than a legal contract, whose friendship was genuine. He was the essence of small, hometown America.

But a part of Harry was also beyond Rockland, a portion of his heart, of his soul. That part was forever in Berlin, Germany, at the 1936 Olympics.

This was the famous Olympics presided over by an over-confident Adolf Hitler, quickly put in his place by a black American, Jesse Owens, who won the gold and proved wrong Hitler's Aryan race baloney.

Harry Jackson might have won a medal, too, but he never got to go to Berlin, missing qualification in the three-mile run by just seconds. His coach applauded that near-win, correctly labeling Harry as a true winner anyway, this young man from a small community who developed his speed and stamina by delivering milk and mowing lawns and digging graves.

But Harry saw it another way: "I wanted to go to Berlin," he said. Harry would mutter that phrase within probably every day of his life until his passing.

Such was Harry Jackson's dream, and who among us does not also have a dream not realized?

But this man did realize dreams fulfilled. The Rockland Hall of Famer ran 680 races, winning 250 and coming in second or third in most of the others. He raised a fine family. He had a good home life with his wife, Carolyn. The untimely loss of his son Harry Jr., as fine a person as his father, was impossible to take, but Harry Jackson did not let that deep wound prevent him from being a father to Gene and Betty, grandfather to eight and great-grandfather to three.

Once, now so long ago, Harry Jackson carved out the final resting place for Daniel Beard of Suffern, founder of the Boy Scouts of America. That was at Brick Church Cemetery, where Harry's earthly remains will lie for eternity.

But not his soul and spirit. They are already in Sacramento, at the continuing U.S. Olympic Track and Field Trials. Harry will also be at every future Olympic track event.

His broad and engaging grin will be evident; his spiked track shoes will be laced tight; and he will have his usual starting block advantage.

In the late 1930s, Harry Jackson showed my father, Arthur Jr., a runner for Spring Valley High School, how to lean forward like a leopard ready to spring, in the wooden blocks used for track starters.

Harry Jackson is again ready to leap forward as he did daily in his earthly existence.

(July 18, 2000)

John Sutter built newspaper

Jack is watching me write this, so I better do it right.

In fact, my late boss, John A. Sutter, also watched us here at The Journal News. Watched all day. Nights, too. The man was everywhere – in the Nyack newsroom, pushing copy to make deadline; in the composing room, making sure the type was rolled into printing mats; in the West Nyack pressroom, seeing that the editions got off right. Watching everywhere, with great interest, great energy and sometimes with a scowl, was this longtime general manager and vice president.

Jack was also watching the front office the day yet another mailroom employee was hired, in March 1964, when I signed on as a "fly-boy," catching newspapers as they came off the press. I thank him for scribbling his OK on the job application.

As longtime chief honcho here, Jack was watching as we multiplied circulation six times over from 1947, the year he joined the newspaper as a "combination man" or writer/photographer, to 1976, when he retired.

Jack was watching as we went to true countywide coverage; as Rockland, the suburb, began to burst at the seams with more homes, more schools, more businesses, more readers; as we built a pressroom in West Nyack in 1960s; as the paper converted to a modern, offset printing process in 1971; and as we began the Rockland Sunday newspaper in 1972.

As a reporter in the late 1940s, he was one of the first to get a byline on his work, with most staffers not being so recognized. His important stories on sewering needs in Orangetown led to major improvements and encouraged Norman Baker and then reporter R. Clinton Taplin to write a series on countywide sewer needs and editorials that led to prizes and the first (and only) county sewer district.

Most of all, I remember Jack as a hands-on, no-holds-barred, old-fashioned newspaperman who would tell you just what he thought. Red face and penetrating stare included. No minced words. He could and would praise work that he thought was on target, but if you were writing about Rocklanders, you had better get the history right.

Indeed, Jack Sutter was a dyed-in-the-wool Rocklander who eventually moved to South Carolina to be near his daughter and her family, but who continued to write so many letters to quite a few of us still here in Rockland and so frequently that you knew he wanted to stay in touch with the only place he ever called "home."

We staffers at The Journal News sometimes received the wrath of one John A. Sutter because he could explode if need be. Those were less politically correct days, and you could get dressed down mighty fast. And Jack had his particular political feelings and personal beliefs as well, so if you did not mesh with those, sometimes he let you know.

But what he sought most, beyond all personal concerns, was to get out a newspaper full of reports to a hungry Rockland, without fail and on time. His enthusiasm and absolute loyalty to this newspaper were such that even now, 23 years after he last worked here, the man's legacy is not forgotten. Even some of the newer arrivals ask about him.

Just before Jack died Friday at 78 after a final heart attack, he wrote what turned out to be his last letter to me. He had a habit of cheering many of us on. In all his letters, he always made it a point to ask how I was doing. I especially needed and appreciated his counsel after my mother passed away in January.

Jack probably was not feeling well when he wrote that letter, but you would not know it in his prose. He just got up each day and did the job, in that old German family tradition. Without complaint. That's the way his wife, Evelyn, is, too.

He was a friend who was always watching, for our own good and surely for that of this paper. The modern Journal News and many of us are indebted to him.

(March 9, 1999)

Mildred Rippey's soul

To have known Mildred Post Rippey is to have lived, walked, talked and otherwise communed with one of the strongest of human river currents: an engaging soul. Mildred, who died last week at 94 in her beloved Palisades community, charted the rough waters and led us into calm pools through her descriptive poetry, her zest for study and her great giving to those she called her friends.

This writer was privileged to be in his own small canoe almost a decade and a half ago, when I first began penning this column and Mildred, who savored words as much as she loved her area of South Orangetown, contacted me.

Over the years she would call me, write me, invite me to her gatherings and otherwise attempt, often with much success, to cheer me on, to urge me to head for deeper, though often more turbulent, waters.

If some who knew Mildred Post Rippey are less wet behind the ears and bathing more deeply in human understanding, it is due to her.

She, too, was a writer, publishing "Reflections," a book of poetry, in 1985 and in 1973 receiving from Rockland Community College a poetry award. But Mildred talked little of her own work, indeed not much of her own existence at all. She wanted to focus on *you*, and so many of us selfishly let her do that.

Yet Mildred achieved much in life, as a person, as a mother, a worker, a volunteer, a churchwoman. She was the oldest graduate of Rockland Community College, obtaining a degree at 81 with an "A" average. She continued to take studies beyond that, which is not surprising given her fascination with books. Mildred was a librarian at the Palisades Free Library, and she remarked that second to the hamlet of Palisades, her daily sojourn at the library gave her soul its nutrition.

The walls of the quaint library, lined with books old and new, the deep, wood smell of its shelves, the varied patrons and the old table that George Washington had used, set near where she worked, urged Mildred to soak deeply in a daily quiet that re-fortified her.

She would often say that Palisades was her life. She was born there in 1901 to the noted Post family and grew up among the fields, woods, old homes and ancient church (Palisades Presbyterian) that still give Palisades almost an English countryside charm. Whatever thoughts she formed as a young girl, before schooling and during it, whatever pangs and joys of maturity set upon her in young adulthood, whatever trials and tribulations faced her (and she them) in her growing life with extended family, and whatever challenges, accommodations and heights of living met her daily as she lived well into older age, all sprang from the outer soul that is Palisades.

Now Mildred Post Rippey has gone on to join others she once knew in this world, and my guess is that at this moment, she's back at the Palisades Library for her nourishment, or maybe on the bus to RCC's Nyack center or perhaps reading in that comfortable chair of hers, in a home she would never change.

I also hope that she will continue to nudge those of us who need and appreciate her encouragement.

(February 28, 1995)

Molly and 'Duvid,' educators

The scene was always the same: a good-sized man, shrunk a bit by age and lifelong habits of particular posture, seated at an old, wooden kitchen table, elbow resting on the top, a glass of seltzer from the spray bottle in his hand. "Hello, boychick, how's by you?" was David Weissman's usual question.

In the Hillcrest of the mid-1950s, on Karnell Street where I lived, families were beginning to move into the newly built Kuperman Cape Cods, and most of these were Jewish. David Weissman, or "Duvid," as the Yiddish translation went, came by way of the Lower East Side, the garment district, with his wife Molly, his daughter Edith Rittberg and his grandsons Matthew and Arnold. They knew the area from Spring Valley's summer resort days, which were then coming to a close as once summer dwellers became permanent residents. The Thruway and Palisades Interstate Parkway were opening up the area for commuting.

I was friends in my youth with Matthew and, as was usually the case in those days with people on your street becoming your extended family (we all had numerous "adopted" mothers), I was invited into what was to prove a lifelong learning laboratory of Jewish ideas and culture.

First, there was Molly, in her 70s, a Polish immigrant whose half-broken English never got in the way of communicating her Sholom Aleichem wit and understanding of life. In time, whether Matthew was home or not, I would be called in to sit in a chair in the doorway of her bedroom, where she and I would talk about "life."

What did I know of life as a sixth-grader? Nothing, but this wise, now elderly lady, understood that I should not be totally ignorant and. without fanfare, without lecture, with a little pushing and cajoling, Molly introduced me to thought and human understanding.

Whatever prejudices one might have had about people, Jewish people in particular, were hard to keep after those sessions. In fact, all you saw was Molly Weissman, the wise person. I do not know how anti-Semitism develops, but for me it never had a chance after the sessions with Molly.

David Weissman was a different sort, not as deeply philosophical as Molly, but more the practical, down-to-earth individual. Doubtless this was so because of his years as a founder and labor organizer in the

International Ladies Garment Workers Union. He had to be tough and, though his battles were by then over (he was then in his 60s and lived into his 90s), his grasp of life's obstacles was still very keen. His take on things, from the perspective of a sixth-grader, was that you could philosophize about life, about whether it might rain on your parade, but you also better have an umbrella in case it did.

A man of few words, Duvid chose them carefully, and since they were honed, they hit their mark. He was truly an example of the less said the better and how one's tight editing of soapbox topics got you more listeners.

Today, when I sit down myself and have a glass of seltzer (another acquired custom), Duvid Weissman's image is not far behind. Nor is Molly Weissman's. They continue to be lifelong teachers.

(June 18, 1996)

The Melones of Tappan

Every community has its "songwriters," those who compose through deed, example and other influences, enduring, perceptive themes that are the background "music" against which we all live and work.

Not all hear the music, of course, indifferent as some are to the areas in which they reside.

Others may not be aware of this music, so well woven it can be into the tapestry of ordinary things, the comings and goings of what we do day after day. But let the songs stop, and it is as if chirping birds had suddenly flown off. The quiet is in the extreme, and we note their loss.

Tappan, that historic hamlet that figures in so much of our nation's history, and, of course, in this Rockland of nearly 200 years, has its own musical themes. It has, for example, heard the death-march cadence for Maj. John André, convicted as a British spy in 1780. And there was fife and drum for Sir Guy Carleton's meeting with Gen. George Washington at the first British recognition of this new nation in 1783.

Commerce passing though Tappan and southern Rockland in the 1800s, as we and this nation grew with steadiness and steadfastness, and the many visitors at Mabie's Tavern, now the '76 House, added to the sounds of Tappan. These could be heard by any resident, any traveler.

In this century, in the 1940s, when the entire world worried that a second international war would consume us all, thousands of troops bound for the European Theatre of war, many never to return, brought a fervent tempo to the hamlet's song as they moved from Camp Shanks. After the war, the music's intensity increased greatly as suburbia came to Tappan and the surrounding areas.

The orchestration could have become frenetic, the music could have become noise were it not for concerned people like Paul and Betty Melone of Tappan, who would be the new songwriters for the hamlet.

They waltzed in with optimism, with a well-tuned ear for more modern things but also with respect for the music of those who came before them. They came with the class of Bizet, the elegance of Duke Ellington and the snappiness of Glenn Miller.

Paul and Betty were hip moderns ready to live in the "country," but not ready, never ready, to seek the usual changes and makeovers that suburban growth can bring. No abrupt tune swings for them.

Paul and Betty would make music here, yes. They and others like them would reinvigorate the hamlet with fresh themes, such as the beginnings of the Tappan Library and the Hickory Hill homes development. But they also realized that this historic place offered enduring scores – houses seen by Washington and a watershed that served Native Americans, for example. Instead of throwing away the old music, they listened carefully to its notes, those of the past, and incorporated them, with emphasis, in today's music, for today's listeners.

In this way, many have come to know for the first time, for all time it is hoped, the principal theme song of Tappan, that of its history.

Paul and Betty are to be honored this Friday at the 32nd Annual Dinner of the Tappantown Historical Society for many years of community service (at the '76 House, fittingly). The musical selections of that evening should include standards, but the real songs of Tappan have long been played every day in the hamlet because of these two activists.

The community owes a debt of gratitude to the Melones for getting us to listen.

(October 14, 1997)

Wilfred B. Talman

Rockland's official bicentennial activities are coming to an end, but the book should not be closed without a look at the Wilfred Blanch Talman chapter.

The late historian was the father of history reportage in 20th-century Rockland. A journalist and lifelong student of history, Talman passed away at the age of 81 in 1986. He was a direct descendant of Douwe Harmanse Talma, a Dutch trader who traveled up to Rockland in 1675 from New Amsterdam and then decided to stay. A working journalist for more than a half a century, Wilfred Talman worked for the Nyack Evening Journal (predecessor of the Rockland Journal-News), the old Brooklyn Eagle, The New York Times, the Orangetown Telegram and the Rockland Independent.

His classic book, "How Things Began in Rockland County and Places Nearby" (1977), is a collection of columns on local history. It is a book that I would not be without professionally and personally. I have borrowed ideas from it for my own columns and research editorials. And when I read the book for pleasure, I happily visit the Rockland roots of "people, customs, language and manners of living during the early times in a border county of New York State."

Sometimes, I recall a Talman column because I originally read it in the old Rockland Leader, a Spring Valley weekly.

Rockland has some fine histories, including the "History of Rockland County, N.Y.," by the Rev. David Cole (1884); Dr. Frank B. Green's "The History of Rockland County" (1886); "Now and Then and Long Ago in Rockland County" by Cornelia F. Bedell (1941); and various specific books on Camp Shanks, the Haverstraw brick industry, etc.

But for a definitive overview of many things past, the Wilfred Talman book is the best. His pieces capture the flavor of Rockland in its many stages, and in reading them you come to understand how the complex fabric of this county has been woven.

When Wilfred Talman passed on, his son, educator Peter, described the father as "a small-town newspaperman. That was his real love." Wilfred Talman echoed this in his foreword to "How Things Began...," noting that the "original writing and typesetting (of the collected newspaper columns) were done under casual country newspaper practice. Capitalization, punctuation and orthography (spelling usage) have been only mildly conformed with in the text."

No explanation needed. If Talman's pieces are representative of the connection to history that community newspapers must make, and they surely are, then they are most valuable. Their small-town newspaper feel makes them even more so.

I have not heard Wilfred B. Talman's name mentioned enough in this nearly completed celebration of Rockland's 200 years. Yet if it were not for this dedicated local historian, so much of what we have been hearing about, reading about and seeing reenacted would not have been accurately portrayed.

(September 22, 1998)

Rosemarie's calm help

When we are children, we create worlds with limited dimensions, though our imaginations have no boundaries within those walls. That sounds contradictory, but if you see a youngster as craving security, which a child does, you understand the necessary limits of his world. The young person can still soar from within, as long as there is a tether to the imaginary ride so a safe return to the takeoff spot can be ensured.

When I was a smaller person, living at that time in the early 1950s in a bungalow rented from Mrs. Markow off Old Nyack Turnpike in south Spring Valley, I would venture off to visit my friend Harold Rickley, who was encamped in his two-family home off Central Avenue, across from the original Central Ford showroom.

It seemed that every time I went to see Harold, he had moved, either upstairs or downstairs, depending on which part of the house the renter of the moment wanted. On one particular visit, he was living downstairs, and a group of us, including Rosemarie Strippoli and another young girl (maybe 11) whose name I do not recall, had decided to play hide and seek, a very popular game for third-graders. (It was replaced in firth grade by summer canasta games and the more important and ever more satisfying "spin the bottle" sessions in the backyard at my next home off Karnell Street in Hillcrest.)

Harold and his friends were bouncy sorts, full of vim and vigor, and it took all the energy I had left after bicycling two miles from Old Nyack Turnpike to keep up with them.

So, this hide and seek game was particularly fast, with Harold hiding, as it turned out, behind a large refrigerator in the expansive downstairs kitchen. For some reason, be it divine inspiration, a hunch or luck, I figured that the ice box was Harold's hideout and started to open the back door to tag him.

But Rosemarie's friend, who was in the kitchen, ran right past Harold and flung open the door just as I was raising my right hand to get in. The door went one way and my hand the other, right through a large glass pane.

Blood instantly flowed, and Rosemarie, calm Rosemarie amid all the shouting and hysterics, simply grabbed it, squeezed the wound and got me quickly across the street to her house. There her mom, a nurse, knew that I needed stitches. She also knew that my grandfather, Arthur Sr., worked next door as foreman for the old Briarcraft Smoking Pipe factory, so she called over and alerted him.

He took me to see Dr. Selman in downtown Spring Valley, where I was stitched up. I later rode my bike home with one hand, a thrill actually, and I was happy enough since there was not much pain and I didn't have to do anything more than light schoolwork in Miss Rouy's South Main Street School class for a week or two.

It was just a minor childhood accident, which could have happened to any of us or been caused by any of us. It took place within the confines of a neighborhood and among some of its young residents, in our own little world of the moment.

The memory of it has never been painful, and now, when I look at the scar that is still there, I cannot fail to recall one time in the lives of a few good people. And I always think of calm and certain Rosemarie Strippoli, who is now, I am told, equally calm and certain as art coordinator for the South Orangetown School District.

(December 8, 1998)

Coach Thompson: Humanity

The 1990s vogue is to have hands-on education, to get the teacher involved in every facet of a student's life so that the youngster's needs, all 645 of them, are met. It's an impossible job that one person should never be expected to tackle, and it sets aside the disappearing art of self-responsibility, including not making excuses and trying to overcome one's handicaps. But the mission continues because it is politically correct to play to the individual.

Well, years ago, in the later season of a coaching career that helped many a student without a forced hand, I came upon one Herbert Thompson. By the time my brother Craig and I had him as a teacher, along with other third-graders at the old South Main Street School in Spring Valley in 1952, Coach Thompson had left the high school track team.

Left in part because after World War II, all those teachers who held only "normal school" certificates were deemed no longer worthy of big-time education. No matter that they taught well, thank you, during the Depression. No matter that their years of experience would today grant them college credit even beyond the bachelor's and master's degrees now standard.

Coach Thompson, by then a gentle man and a gentleman (there are tales of a "tougher" fellow in earlier incarnations as a football and track coach), was pushed by the bureaucracy and by dint of what some thought "modern" education should demand, into the lower grades, first into the South and North Main Street schools and then into girls' coaching.

He did not complain, for it was not his way, and besides, he never had the stomach to fight officialdom. No, he just kept at his work, making sure every youngster got out on the field, seeing that the loose energy that could become fistfights and bloody noses was redirected into hitting the ball.

Coach Thompson never gave orders; never barked at his young charges. He did not see school gym as a military exercise. Even as a track coach, as my father tells me (he was a runner at the old Spring Valley High School in the 1930s), Thompson, with some exceptions, was not overbearing but urged the team on as a group of individuals (because that is what track sports are, individuals working together).

I did not know him in that season. I met him after his life was forever changed by the loss of a son in World War II and during what had to be trying days as education itself changed.

Let's not second-guess those standards, for we must, generally, have improving ones, in education and in other fields. But sometimes the rules and regulations reject the really talented people whose work surpasses the goals that are actually being sought in the changes. They are sacrificed to progress.

Coach Herbert Thompson gave me, gave my brother, my father and countless boys (and girls) lessons in the dignity of life, school work and being human.

I'd say that made him a Doctor of Humanity.

(March 21, 1995)

Norm Baker's copy rhythm

Norm Baker was the sort of editor whose gas tank was forever full, but you did not always hear the motor running. Except when he was pushed to the limit by a particular cause or difference with a fellow editor, reporter or reader, he kept quiet and close to the task at hand: putting out The Journal News in the 1930s to the 1960s.

In those days before the Computer Age came to newspapers too, we were major purchasers of the heavy-lead copy pencil. We did our page designs or "dummies" with it; we wrote assignment notes with it; and, of course, we edited copy with these wide-lead pencils. Norm Baker used them too, really used them, to the point, literally, of wearing them down to 3-inch size, sometimes even less.

He was of the "use it up, don't throw it out" mentality so common in the Great Depression. The paper probably also had a pretty tight budget for supplies.

You would find Norm at the old horseshoe-shaped copy desk, the "rim," in the "slot," or area facing the other editors lined about the rim. In rolled-up, white shirtsleeves, maybe with a bow tie, his furrowed brow topped a face set with glasses that presented him overall as "bookish." He sat rather straight up, not hunched over like so many other editors, bowed into characteristic pose by demands of close, curse-filled copy editing in dim light.

Cigarette lit, reading copy and following it line by line with his pencil, Norm would hide the small pencil in his fingers, tarrying at this line or that, inserting a word or crossing out some, with all action barely noticeable.

He would go on for hours like this, with the fuel tank emptying but the engine so quiet and the hand movement with the hidden copy pencil so light that you hardly noticed.

Sometime in mid-afternoon, Norm would get up from the slot and walk off without saying a word, head out the heavy, metal front door at the old newspaper building at 53 Hudson Ave. in Nyack and walk down to Broadway and Arnold's luncheonette (later Elliot's and then the present Strawberry Place). There, he would invariably refuel the tank with a scrambled egg on white, not toasted. And, of course, coffee, befitting the newsmen of the time, who generally could not get through the day without java and tobacco (as well as some of the harder stuff for more than enough of the tribe).

In the early 1960s, Norm concentrated on the Editorial Page, where as one of my predecessors, he distinguished himself by copping the first-place award from the New York State Publishers Association for a series of editorials on the need to set up a county sewer district. His writings, dating from the days when he took over for chief editor Walter Williams in 1940, were noted for their emphasis on what could improve the quality of Rocklanders' lives in a growing, changing suburbia.

Norm Baker is largely unsung these days because fewer are left to recall his tenure. Most of my time under his editorship was spent first as a copyboy (Norm hired me in 1964 after I had previously worked in the pressroom) and then as a staff photographer for 6-plus years. So, he did not edit much of what little copy I produced. Yet, the image of him sitting quietly amidst the traditional din of a newsroom, copy pencil barely visible under hand, rhythm all his own, stays in the brain to this day and, from time to time, jogs the memory of one of the longtime editors of this newspaper. (April 15, 1997)

A Rockland treasure

The news article said Helen Hayes, or Mrs. Charles MacArthur of Nyack, is going to receive the Medal of Freedom.

It's the highest civilian award in the nation, and it's going to be presented by the president. Heady stuff, but not unusual for the First Lady of the American Stage. Now almost 86, she has garnered more accolades from presidents and potentates, on the stage and on tour, than there are flowers in her considerable – and beautiful – garden.

Helen Hayes surely will receive the medal, at White House ceremonies later this month, with the same quiet dignity that has been her life's companion and with enthusiasm equal to a child getting her first doll. You'd think she'd be used to big awards by this time, but not Mrs. MacArthur.

Now this is a presumption, but a pretty safe one. You see, I met Helen Hayes just once, and talked only briefly with her, but in that short encounter, I had the privilege of *reading* her face. There's a lot of story there.

First, it's a kind face, and it is no mask. There's a graciousness about the woman and a true concern and interest in others, no matter who the person may be.

It's an Irish face, and the gritty determination to do things just so and to be stubborn where it counts is evident.

It's a face that does not hide sadness, but which does not ask you to feel sorry. Its beautiful lines have absorbed unexpected grief, since you do not endure the loss of a husband and a daughter without feeling it from head to toe.

It's a face that has seen kings, has played a queen and has looked on the flagstone sidewalks along Broadway in her village. The emotions called for in each of these situations – courtesy, regality and homespun warmness – have poured forth from the same face, easily, because it is this woman's nature to be genuine, whether she is an actress or one of us.

It's a face that has seen the brightest Broadway lights and the dimmest of seasons. It is a face that has recited countless lines countless times, with enough dialogue memorized that she could play any part at a moment's notice.

And it's a face that often gazes on a garden overlooking the Hudson River, reflecting her love for the simple beauty of flowers.

It was there – in her garden – that I met Helen Hayes, having been assigned in the late 1960s by this newspaper to take her picture. The assignment went along quickly as Miss Hayes, naturally, cooperated in the posing. I had taken a few pictures and was about to shoot the last frame when I looked up and noticed her face. It was a fast moment, but what I saw told me much.

Miss Hayes' face is not unlike her flowers – it has simple, honest, but deep, beauty.

A treasure, really.

(May 6, 1986)

Burgess Meredith's touch

Most of the usual has been said about Burgess Meredith, late of Rockland and this good Earth. Noted in the fine obituaries and tributes have been his films, his contributions to village formation in Pomona and his association with the thespian literati. But what about the man himself, the inner core?

While this writer cannot possibly define his own inner core, much less anyone else's, I can tell you of one encounter with Burgess Meredith that may speak of the man's heart and soul.

Back in 1967, just as the Committee for the Incorporation of the Village of Pomona had won its public vote against strong opposition by Ramapo and Haverstraw politicos, the first mayor, Jan H. Van den Hende, told Meredith about the massive legal debt left by the fight.

The actor, famous for fine performances in such Broadway plays as "Winterset" and "High Tor" and his movies, offered to allow his large estate to be used for a fund-raising horse show. He did this even though he was not a resident of the village but, rather, lived just across from the old Camp Hill School, now Village Hall.

The new mayor accepted and the event attracted 15,000 people, way more than the 3,000 hoped for. There were notables galore, such as Lauren Bacall, and Meredith wore his Penguin character suit from "Batman." He did most of his own publicity through a network of well-placed friends and a two-week guest stint as co-host of the "Today Show." But, still, the Rockland Journal-News sent me to do a pre-publicity photo of the actor.

I got to his estate, off Quaker and Camp Hill roads, and found Meredith in the middle of his grazing field. He had on jodhpurs, and he and a horse were tethered to each other by the reins. I should have been nervous, but on that particular day, my then-photo chief, Al Witt, had loaded me up with six assignments, and I had just a few minutes for this shot. So, I had to get the job done, and there was no time for a bad case of the nerves.

I need not have worried anyway. Burgess Meredith was a most obliging fellow, ready for the camera and willing to take direction as the shot was set up. He, with a bit of help from me, got onto the horse and we got the picture.

I realize that actors are used to cameras and taking direction, but he did not have to be as decent as he was. He could have tried to bulldoze the session, to make it what he wanted it to be (that would not have worked, though). Or, he could have been syrupy and pushed the PR baloney in hope of getting bigger play in the paper (no go there, either).

Yet, he took neither course. Burgess Meredith was an extraordinary Joe sincerely living the real life part of an ordinary fellow.

He had class.

The same observation of likeability and good neighborliness was made by my colleague Grant Jobson, former Editorial Page editor, who occasionally bumped into Meredith on the job or when Burgess and his actor pal Franchot Tone spent time at drinking spots in Mount Ivy. And, my father, who as a young fellow delivered newspapers to Meredith, also reports that he was a decent person.

So, let us note that, too, in Burgess Meredith's life, along with the usual facts of Hollywood notoriety.

(September 23, 1997)

Martio, pizza man/counselor

An obituary, or the account of one's passing and of a life now gone, rarely tells the whole story, and even more rare is it that the essence of the individual is captured. Yet the retelling of one's time on Earth can offer gems of insight, character, understanding, excitement, intrigue, drama and humor.

Obit writing is for the most gifted of newspaper wordsmiths, though far too many papers give the duty short shrift. Space, finances, tastes all dictate these final stories of loved ones, leaders and the forgotten soul.

So, there are fewer stories told, and the human experience is the lesser for that.

It is left to the reader to fill in the blanks, and we can at least do that if we knew the one who has passed. For even in the quick reading of the obit page, as one tends to do every day as we age, a memory can be triggered, and we who were acquainted with the individual can recall him or her and write our own obit of that soul.

Such was the case recently when numerous Rocklanders, including this Spring Valleyite of the 1950s, caught the name Frank Colandrea, 67, of the Valley, in the obit listings.

No one we knew ever called this man Frank. He was "Martio," the man who brought sliced pizza to Rockland and Spring Valley (1958).

He was just 24 then, and together with a beautiful wife, Lois, they built Martio's into a great pizza parlor that constantly attracted many across Rockland.

The store became an after-school haunt, a weekend spot, surely a summer place.

Before Martio's arrival, Rockland knew nothing about sliced pizza, save those newer arrivals from New York City's boroughs where such a treat had long been deliciously on the menu.

But in Rockland, the only pizza we had before 1958 and the growing suburban push was "pizza pie," the tavern-made round or square, thick- or thin-crust pizza that took 20 minutes to make.

You might call beforehand to order the pizza pie for take-out, as my father used to do with the great tavern pie from Nanuet Hotel and also from the Nanuet Restaurant. Or you could go in person, say to Perruna's, in the Valley, which had the best thin-crust pie, or to Bartero's, farther down Main Street, which made a Sicilian-type square pie with heavy crust.

Martio's brought a new recipe to town. There, as in so many succeeding pizza parlors to crop up in Rockland (there must be 50 now), the pizza was made in 10 minutes and could be had by the slice.

Martio charged 15 cents a slice in 1958, and because we teens could once and a while manage that cost easier than the price of a tavern pie, we flocked to Martio's. The pizza was different, not the deeper, perhaps richer taste of the tavern pie, with its secret family recipes (can anyone duplicate the pizza in Nanuet?), but the 10-minute pie was also quite good.

Of course, the taste would depend on the maker and the taster, and some pizza parlors then, as now, do a better job, use more expensive cheese, richer sauce and well-crafted dough, etc.

Bottom line at Martio's in Spring Valley, 1958: The pizza was very good. But even better was the atmosphere. Youngsters need a place to gather, and Martio gave us that.

He kept his Main Street storefront, just up from St. Joseph's Church, very clean. He tolerated no wise guys or trouble.

And he and his wife offered more than a few youngsters a kind word when they were down, a free slice and reassurance that life can be good.

Martio would eventually leave the Valley, and in 1975 he and his family opened a stylish restaurant-pizza parlor in Nanuet. It has become a fixture on its own for generations of Rocklanders.

When I was last there a few weeks ago, I spotted Martio, the once-24-year-old, as I was paying the bill. Quieter, grayer, slower, his eyes were concentrating on what must have been the one-millionth turn of the ladle of sauce against rolled-out dough.

What had he thought about in all those turns in all those years? How many kids had he talked to in kindness? How much happiness had he delivered in a slice of pizza?

Martio is gone now, though the family legacy continues. His obituary that ran on July 20 gave basic details, but unless you knew Martio, you could not understand the gifts this man served a growing suburban Rockland and its teens. The memories he provided so many of us will do that. They will write his real obit.

(July 31, 2001)

Promise still unfolds

Forty years ago now, Nov. 19, 1960, Spring Valley High School, Class of '61, lost a classmate, Fred Yatto Jr., just 17. He was the school's General Organization president and popular with students. Fred was everyone's friend, and his ability to get along with people proclaimed great promise for his future.

But, just as he was about to add school sports to his busy schedule, a routine physical detected an unusual sound in his heart. Further investigation revealed a hole, possibly begun by a cold virus some years before. This meant open-heart surgery, then in its infancy and far, far riskier than what is now the norm.

Fred knew his surgery was coming up in early November 1960, but he tried to make light of it, hoping not to worry his classmates and friends, many of whom were into the usual fall madness of football, the last year in high school, college applications and what would prove to be the final season for our school's longtime principal, Leland Rickard-Meyer.

Besides, most of us were too immature and inexperienced in death to know the very grave danger Fred faced. He knew that.

On Nov. 12, Fred presided over a pre-football game ceremony on the new field off Route 59 in which Gerd Bitten Andersen, our Danish exchange student, was recognized.

And about two weeks before his surgery, he went to a party in Pomona with some friends, this writer included. The small amount of alcohol he had there, in his condition, caused him to pass out. We carried him onto a bed in a spare room at Joan Prescott's Pomona Road home so he could recover.

It was a prescient moment.

Just a few weeks later, some of us would again carry Fred Yatto, this time to his final resting place on this Earth, the West New Hempstead Cemetery just a few miles from the Prescott house. Fred died Nov. 19, 1960, after the open-heart operation revealed a hole the size of a half-dollar, and in those days it could not be repaired successfully.

When our classmate passed away, so ended the innocence of school life for the Class of '61. We have had other classmates leave us too soon in later years, but Fred was the first, and he died all too young particularly.

The good times eventually returned to SVHS, but the black fact that death comes to us all, including the young, was forever imprinted on our psyche. It changed us, some for life. The journeys each of us have taken from Nov. 19, 1960 have been set in part by that fact.

When I visit Fred's grave at New Hempstead, I also pay my respects to Josef Bernard, our fellow classmate whose remains lie not far from Fred's. And I stop by the graves of John and Marie Romaine, Harry Jackson and so many others whose families defined Spring Valley and/or SVHS. Fred surely has great company.

Each of these people has had an effect on my life and on countless others. I thank them for that.

As for Fred, while I know that, in an earthly view, he was denied the right, the joys, even the sorrows of life beyond high school, into middle and old age, and the effects of a job, a career, family and so much more; and while his mother Selma, his brothers, Robert and Thomas, and his late father, Fred Sr., also lost the physical presence of a fine young man of promise, it must be stated that the spirit of Fred Yatto has lived a life.

He has lived it and continues to live it, in his friends and former classmates, who, once in a while, reflect on the young man who was and the man who should have been.

I recall his eagerness, his humor, his sense of responsibility, his very love for life.

What were to be his hopes, his aspirations, his ups and downs, have been experienced in some way or another by the Class of '61. Some of us have thought, what would Fred have said about this or that, or what would he have done in such and such a moment (especially in this interesting presidential election; he loved politics).

The realization that some 40 years later, a 17-year-old fellow is not forgotten is proof that a life did not end on this earth on Nov. 19, 1960. (Oct. 31, 2000)

John Romaine: Individualist

Earlier in this American century, there were individuals in Rockland and elsewhere, of course, who were, well, individuals. These were pioneering people in the crafts, arts and sciences who took inspiration from the great inventors of the later 1800s and early 1900s: Thomas Edison, Alexander Graham Bell, Guglielmo Marconi and Lee DeForest.

Every town in the United States had these people, garage tinkerers who followed Edison's dictum, that to invent, to advance in any self-taught area, requires one percent inspiration and 99 percent perspiration. They gave us the many defining moments of great invention that have made our life easier in this, the 20th century.

One fellow of note in this bunch was Spring Valleyite John E. Romaine, who long resided on Church Street and then on Locust Street, Hillcrest, just up the "Boulevard."

He was a major tinkerer, self-taught in the very early days of radio, acquiring enough knowledge that he could operate his own business, Ro-Field Appliances on Main Street, near the corner of Church, for many years and then run a TV and radio repair shop out of his Hillcrest home. In his final working years, he was still at the trade, but at Rockland Community College where he assisted in the audiovisual department.

Over those many decades from the 1920s until the 1970s, John Romaine was a teacher, even if he did not know it. Young fellows would come into his shop to get replacement batteries for the large portable radios that were in use before the transistor was invented.

He was careful to show them how the radio was put together and to reveal the inner workings.

On a visit to his home, he would more often than not grab a piece of scrap paper and quickly sketch for a visitor a simple schematic for the five-tube basic radio, explaining in clear terms how the vacuum tube invented by DeForest and others worked to amplify and modulate and filter these mysterious, unseen radio waves that could carry voices.

In these lessons, delivered with the graciousness of a kindly, friendly man, he was still teaching himself. Indeed, John Romaine was a lifelong self-instructor, and that was the source of his working inspiration.

It was also the basis for a business that provided for his wife, Marie, son, John Jr., and daughter, Lucille. The son would go on to become an electrical engineer, learning on the master's degree level all the theory that his father had never absorbed. He was successful in his own right, but it was John Romaine Sr. to whom the son turned when there was a problem with a radio or TV, for it was the father who had the practical experience.

Practical experience obtained from 99 percent perspiration.

So many others have followed this route in this century, redefining our lifestyles and making great advances in medicine, the automotive world, home construction and other quality-of-life areas. These individuals went about their work with diligence and self-discipline, and no corporation, no matter how well-organized, no matter how well-staffed, could beat that, for the inspiration that gave us so much.

The John Romaines of this century made it what it is, in Rockland and elsewhere.

(Oct. 11, 1999)

Section Two
Rockland Places

Watching the 6:45

It was wartime. Ration books for gasoline, food, clothes. No tires for your car. Blackout restrictions. Air raid spotters, air raid drills. Few young men to be seen. Factories humming. Women working. Making do with less. Ears cocked to the radio every night. Telegrams from the War Department.

A time of nervous anticipation that someone you knew – or knew of – wouldn't make it. Also days of boredom, because without gas or tires you couldn't go far, not even for a Sunday ride. But there was a job to do and jobs to make sure that was done. At least the war had brought an end to the Depression.

And like any time, any period in history, events of the day determined the *day* and the routine. Clocks set back or forward so the cows and people could produce more, movies made for the range of human emotions then unfurling – patriotism, love, humor, sadness, hope. Scrap drives, blood drives, bond drives.

All this, but you still got up in the morning, still washed your face, still ate dinner, still walked the dog. And if you had grandchildren you might take them with you when you went out.

I lived in Spring Valley during World War II. I was just a tyke in 1944, but something happened to me then, during that time of deprivation, as part of the routine of that day, that made an everlasting impression.

My grandfather did a lot of walking. He had sold his red 1940 Chevrolet to buy his Ternure Avenue home and so hoofed it back and forth, down and up the old brick hill on Route 59 to the Briarcraft smoking pipe factory in the Pipetown section of the village. With all that walking, so you wouldn't think he'd want any more of it after dinner.

But he had grandchildren who were restless, and it was wartime with not much to do and few places to go. No TV top act as babysitter, either.

So, my grandfather, in his routine, would take my brother and me down Ternure and across Central Avenue to the Erie Railroad tracks. My brother and I would try to balance ourselves on the rails while my grandfather took his time some steps behind. Along the way, we would stop at some of the freight cars on the siding, hopping in to roll around in the little bit of cornfeed that was always left in the cars.

Eventually, we would get to the old freight station off Commerce Street and sit in the sun of an August evening, looking across the way at the Comfort Coal yards, the many mounds of coal and the giraffe-like unloaders that took the coal out of the rail cars.

We would remain on the platform for maybe 45 minutes, alternating between sitting, lying down, playing hide and seek and jumping on the tracks. My grandfather would just stare into the distance and keep his usual, quiet ways.

In time, the *big moment* would arrive. My brother and I would stop our playing and my grandfather his staring. We'd all look to the south, our ears quickly following. Peering toward Main Street, our hands under our legs as we sat on the freight platform, we'd see the first burst of steam, then another and another. The sound of the chugging pistons would be heard, in cadence with the bursts of steam.

Around the bend off Lawrence Street, just behind the railroad station, the steam locomotive would chug up a slight grade and hiss to a stop.

Its few passengers let off, the train would continue our way, headed straight for the freight platform. At the very last moment, it would make a wide turn to the right and make for the roundhouse off Union Road and Maple Avenue where the giant locomotive would give up its grunts and groans for its nightly sleep.

The three of us, momentarily lost in steam, would then get up, and my brother and I, running ahead of my grandfather, would head home.

This exercise, this part of the routine in a small village during wartime, would also rest, to be repeated in the repetition that is blessed in such difficulty and experience. Eventually, the memory of all the walks to watch the train would blend into one warm recollection, to be tapped from my past when I need it most.
(February 19, 1983)

A juicy bite of Rockland life

What is a Rockland fall without chomping on one of our famous apples? It's just not as beautiful, that's all.

Apples have grown from trees rooted in the county's rocky soil almost as long as our heritage has been nurtured here. Perhaps we grow such great apples because Rockland is blessed with a combination of earth, weather and the sweat and care of farmers whose hands are guided by the spirits of their ancestors.

They neither could nor would turn out a poor crop, for only doing the best by the land is the credo that lets them sleep in peace after the usual day's hard work. They all hear their fathers and their fathers' fathers telling them that good apples only come from good effort.

I eat apples all year long. I'm convinced the pectin in them helps lower the blood pressure that tends to run high on my mother's side of the family, and I like the flushed face that I get after I bite into the deep red skin of a Rockland Empire or the red side of a MacIntosh.

It's not the flush of a shy person or the red-faced embarrassment of someone caught with his hand in the cookie jar or found day-dreaming in class, but more like the quick glow you get when you come across someone you care for deeply in an unexpected and delightful moment. It is fresh and refreshing.

Cortlands are just fine, too, for variety, as is a native Red Delicious, so unlike the wax-like commercial Red Delicious, which prove mealy.

My apples find their way into pies and applesauce, homemade to be sure, with the aroma always reminding me of grandmother's kitchen and the simple delight of eating a big piece of pie with vanilla ice cream after school. A memory like that can feed you for decades.

I keep apples in a bowl on the kitchen table for the look and the fragrance that greet you at the end of a long day. I also let the drops off my neighbor's crab apple tree cover my lawn and turn to food for worms and insects, because the smell is deep and lasting, enough to get me through the winter.

And I take an apple or two with me on a walk in Chestnut Ridge or Stony Point, up a mountain or along a stream, since a good, crunchy apple can make you think just right, or forget to think at all, if that's your wish.

An apple is an inexpensive way to keep you healthy, physically and mentally. It's handy, for it's not too large that you can't tuck it away in your pocket. It stays fresh for a long time and, most of all for me at least, every bite is a connection with a county in which I feel privileged to live. (October 12, 1993)

When the lights went out

Where were you when the lights went out on Nov. 9, 1965? It's been 20 years since a bad relay in Canada snuffed out power in the Northeast through a series of chain reactions, and maybe a look back is in order.

Rockland, unlike New York City, was not caught in the rush hour when the lights began dimming at 5:28 p.m. since there was no true rush hour. We had few people stuck in elevators because we had few elevators. Traffic was no problem, so we did not need the fine assistance of the citizenry, as happened in New York when motorists jumped from their cars and directed traffic.

Yet Rockland, too, was a model of cooperation and individual genius. In Pearl River, a barber finished a haircut by wedging two candles between the keys of a cash register and had the customer hold a candle in each hand. Scissors took the place of an electric razor.

In Nyack, some areas west of Broadway had lights, and stores there enjoyed better business than usual. Elsewhere in the village, the Fire Patrol used emergency lights to brighten the annual football awards dinner of the Monday Morning Quarterback Club. Suffern police put six extra patrolmen on duty but, as was the case in the rest of Rockland, no untoward incidents were reported. In Clarkstown, officials continued working on the master plan, using flashlights. The power came on at 9:30 p.m., just as the group was leaving.

Low Tor Mountain was brightly lit, not by the usual glow to the south from New York City but from one of the brightest moons of the season. Orangetown averted an overflow at its new sewer plant in Orangeburg by calling in emergency generators to power pumps. Throughout the county, members of the citizens Radio Association of Rockland provided two-way radio communication for people without phone service.

Employees of various stores used car lights to shine through front windows and conduct minimal business. In Nanuet, the Korvettes department store lost power for just a short time and became a mecca for people in the dark with nothing to do.

Lederle Laboratories in Pearl River put its civil defense emergency procedure into effect, and the blackout proved an enlightening experience because the huge chemical complex was able to work out minor kinks in the plan.

Orange & Rockland Utilities was busy, of course, attempting to restore power to various areas of Rockland, but it also found time to perform a unique service when it provided 20,000 kilowatts to Consolidated Edison so that huge power company could get its generators moving again. The upstate central Hudson region was given 10,000 kilowatts.

The county was one of the few areas in the Northeast where power never ceased completely on Nov. 9, 1965, and most service was restored by 8:30 p.m. Things were back to normal just hours after the blackout, but in Rockland, as in New York City, New Jersey and other Northeast areas, that long, black night would provide a topic of conversation for years to come. (November 12, 1985)

The expandable attic

I know the official line will probably be that it isn't cost-effective, or put in a more complex way, that the ratio of land to materials to labor isn't enough to guarantee big bucks, but isn't it time we brought back the expandable attic?

Way back in the post-war days after the last world conflict in Europe and the Pacific, the official bigwigs of this nation were wise enough to support the returning GIs through low-cost mortgages. Housing demand, long stifled by the Great Depression, pent-up during the war years and pushed to the limit by the many war babies, was like a dam ready to burst. The cheaper mortgages helped, but so did the expandable attic.

Builders, like the famous Levitt family in Long Island and the original tract builders in Rockland, realized that homes had to be built quickly and affordably. One way to do that was to put together a Cape Cod with an unfinished attic. One-third of the house was left raw, as was the basement.

Later on, as the family grew and so did wages, the new breed of American do-it-yourself male, assisted (and sometimes surpassed) by his bride, who had learned self-sufficient home skills in the war years, tackled the attic. Sometimes this would take a few years, with Junior and Sis camping out under insulation-covered ceilings, exposed beams and bare lightbulbs. On weekends Dad would take his copy of Family Handyman and put up some sheetrock, or maybe wire an outlet, or staple ceiling tiles or construct a built-in bookcase.

With time out for Groucho Marx's "You Bet Your Life" or the "Jack Benny Show," and kept going by income tax refunds and Mom's glass-jar savings, the project would eventually be finished. The result was often highly individualistic, with some very professionally built attics and others that were sort of just put together.

But no matter. The attics had been *expanded* to meet the needs of a growing family through the limited resources of an emerging family budget. The family ended up with a home much bigger than it could have initially afforded, and as a bonus, it completed a project together. There are many moms and dads out there today who wistfully look back on the days when they and their children sweated out their attic project.

These days, most homes have no usable attics, no loft space that can be converted into unique angular places with a few dollars here and there as family and friends donate time, energy and companionship. Big bucks must be coughed up for a completed house.

We should go back to the expandable attic. Design smaller homes with unfinished space that the American family can complete in sweat and dedication and closeness. You will also cut the cost of the houses in the process and ensure more people a grab at the American Dream.
(June 25, 1991)

Special class, joined in life

Ask a teacher, and the person will tell that you each year's class (Class of 1994, for example) has its unique characteristics. Taken as a whole, the class is either brighter, not as creative, more social, less troublesome, etc. It's almost as if the class has its own astrological sign (guess it does, actually).

This isn't to generalize negatively or positively about any particular class, because in a class, as in this world, individuals do count (otherwise, let's give up now), but on the whole, you are sure to get a certain sense about any one year's class.

I'm prejudiced, of course, about my own Class of 1961, Spring Valley High. I think the class was cast in favorable light when we first assembled here and there, in various Rockland, New York City, and other school systems 13 years before. When we all came together in those final years of high school, there was a flavor that we still call home in our memories.

Ask Sandy Davis (maiden names used here). Or Gene Jackson. Or Tring Butt. Or Mark Broat. Or Lucille Romaine. Or George D'Loughy. Or just about any of us. While you can't expect us to fairly rate our class on its academic skills, or school spirit, or grown-up success rate, or community involvement, or as holding this value or that, because we are partial to our own group, we can tell you that Spring Valley High was a fun place to be in 1958-1961.

The Class of '61, in the toiling that is life, in the emotional ups and downs, in the challenges of family, work and relationships, has its particular anchors, set in the sure footings of well-cast memories.

I've occasionally shared these moments with you during these 14-plus years of writing this column (maybe to a fault). In doing so, as in penning this piece, I have tried to relate my experiences to your experiences and thus spur a pleasant memory jog, since you probably think your own class was special.

I know that I am not alone in remembering our class as a strong moment in our lives. After a lapse of too many years, I ran into Sandy Davis just before Christmas, in the Pearl River bank where she's employed. The seasons have not aged her, and while I recognized the face, I did not immediately recall her name. She filled me in on that and also began to talk in the same stream of consciousness from which my columns drink. It was almost like listening to myself, albeit a much prettier version.

I have met others along the way, over these years since we have left Principal Leland Rickard-Meyer's warm and caring tutelage, since we gave up the Friday night basketball games, the G.O. meetings, school dances, school crushes, school exams. All former classmates report enduring, enjoying, loving and tearing through these many years.

And though we have not seen all that much of each other as our lives have taken us here and there, I'll bet you that if, by dint of some special cosmic circumstance, the homeroom bell should ring once more, we'd quickly find ourselves "home" again at Spring Valley High, with friendships, classes, activities, even dreams and fears renewed in an instant.

Guess we're all brothers and sisters in that way, forever, this Class of 1961.

(January 3, 1995)

Looking at Rockland in 2789

April 29, 2789 – Archaeologists digging in the hollows of West Nyack have unearthed the remains of a 20th century landfill, according to a report in the local newspaper/videotext, The Journal-News. The usual material has been found – plastics and well-rusted metal appliances, leading the experts to categorize the people of 1989 as ordinary in the then-accepted habit of irresponsible waste elimination.

Toxics were found, too, and the entire Hackensack River valley has been cordoned off for a quarantine period: one century. Again, not unusual for an archaeological dig going back to 1989.

Up along Smith Road toward Spring Valley, though, another dig has found even more alarming evidence of what was once man's great indifference to the environment. There, the remains of old washing machines, fuel tanks, rugs and household garbage abound on a site where the ancient maps indicate there was an old airport. From the traffic patterns recreated by looking at the maps, it's obvious that 1989 people pulled up in their station wagons and minivans to dump anything they wished, apparently without conscience, on a site that was not a legal landfill.

There is no record in police or newspaper files of anyone being arrested for the littering, although old photographs indicate that signs were indeed posted, warning of littering and fines upon conviction. Archaeologists even found an old automobile propped up against one of the signs. So much for law and order in the 1980s.

Encouraged by their find, the diggers moved on to Viola Road in Viola, Bradley Parkway in Blauvelt and streets in greater Suffern, Ladentown, Stony Point and Sparkill. Each day, it seems they find more junk, more debris. So much so that social scientists have now joined the digs. Was littering symptomatic of the times, they ask? Did people really dislike their fellow humans so much that they dumped wherever they wanted, regardless of whom it may have hurt?

Was this attitude carried over into other areas of living? Did people cut off others on the highways? Did they steal and cheat? Did some flee urban areas ostensibly because of crime, only to bring another form of crime to the suburbs? Were they joined by Rockland natives too selfish to recognize the value of the precious land on which they lived?

The experts are having a field day with their discoveries. Similar finds have been dug up in other areas of the world, to be sure, but the scientists are increasingly being drawn to Rockland because of the high concentration of litter so far unearthed.

One archaeologist put his finger on all the hoopla when he said, "It appears that the average Rocklander in 1989 saw not evil, heard no evil, spoke no evil, as he drove down the road oblivious to the growing piles of litter about him. Indeed, he usually added to the piles by chucking out a hamburger wrapper or a washing machine."

The question on everyone's mind is how did Rockland survive? (April 29, 1989)

No zoning variance required

Today you would probably need a zoning variance and a flood plain plan, but in pre-Tappan Zee Bridge Rockland (1955), there was much land where a kid could build a hut or tree house. In fact, it was an annual ritual.

I built huts in south Spring Valley, off Old Nyack Turnpike, and in Hillcrest, off Karnell and Hickory streets. In Spring Valley, my hut was made of common straw, the sort that dotted most open fields in the county. We would use tree branches for support, old pieces of wood for doors, a discarded section of glass for a window and the straw and twigs for siding and roofing.

My Valley hut was located just on the edge of what is now the Thruway tollbooth plaza, and I was the only homeowner after my brother Craig, in a fit one year, pulled out of joint ownership, took the front door and built his own hut a bit upfield.

We would spend our third-grade weekends working on the huts, usually in the fall and spring. The structure would be in use until the first snow, and occasionally we would make a small fire to heat a can of Campbell's tomato soup. In the dense quiet of a falling snow, with just a candle or two for light, the hot soup tasted like a meal fit for a king in this palace – a palace because it was our own.

When I moved to Hillcrest in the fifth grade, hut-building was upgraded a notch or two because we had more open land. (Our house was, according to the builder, the last one on the street, but three years later there were 40 more.) We also had access to scrap material – the cast-off framing wood and No. 2 grade pine tongue-and-groove roof-decking scrap that the carpenters left all over their building sites. We even used the cement cast off by the masons.

Some fellows built tree houses, even elaborate ones, but I always favored the lean-to style, constructed on a clearing in the woods. It would go up in a few days, but used as a clubhouse for a week or so and then be dismantled in the childhood rush to go on to something else.

In its time, the hut would provide a home away from home, space in which to think your own thoughts, a place to go when your mother was cleaning the house on a Saturday and you had to get lost. You could jaw in privacy with your pals, play cards, eat treats in a bachelor pad.

But you always made sure to leave when it was dinnertime, because hot tomato soup could only carry you so far. Your mother's cooking was worth the trip home.

(November 20, 1990)

Others have been here

There are enough people in any moment who are sure they have invented the wheel, who believe that those who came before them are of little consequence, that the only thing that matters is the here and now.

Hogwash. They, too, are but a blip on the screen that notes decades and centuries and through which pass the facts of accomplishment and failure. If it all were on video tape, and we all could sit down and watch life as it has unfolded from the beginning, we would see many individuals lay claim to being the first with this or that, or to having a superior civilization unsurpassed by any other. As the tape was fast-forwarded and then reversed, though, we'd find that most everything has been done before, sometimes better. It would be a humbling experience.

That's the sort of feeling you get from reading yesterday's Journal-News story on the discovery of ancient Indian artifacts at Potake Lake in western Ramapo. Some of the finds date back to 3,500 B.C. Imagine, just a few hundred feet a way from the busy traffic on Route 17, near the New York State Thruway and the great mass of civilization that is the metropolitan area, stone weapons and tools were simply lying on the ground, silent witnesses to an era in which people lived, died and toiled in between, just as we do today.

Archaeologist Edward J. Lenik uncovered the artifacts as he walked around the 94-acre Potake Lake, which is part of a planned development of luxury estate homes on a 2,260-acre section of the Ramapo Mountains. The Ramapo Land Co., which owns the lake, says it will preserve the Indian campgrounds and the site might eventually be opened to groups wishing to explore the historic spot.

That's a good idea. There are too many people in this world who are ignorant of the past, who have no taste or regard for what others did before them. The more they can be told about the great – and not-so-great – peoples who came before them, the better the chance for understanding life itself.

The Potake Lake finds were dated by using comparisons from other archaeological finds, and Lenik notes there are 12 or so similar Indian campsites in southeastern New York and northern New Jersey. It's not known what the Indians called themselves, although Munsee (Muncee)-speaking Indians from a Delaware tribe later lived in the area, including what is now Monsey. (Their sandstone caves can be seen in the Monsey Glen off Route 59.)

Lenik adds that "the white man destroyed many of these sites when he settled in this area and took the best land." Ah, that sounds familiar. Developments and shopping centers in Rockland have also taken some of the best land for modern tribes, and the history of the people who lived and thrived in other times has been all but forgotten.

Forgotten, that is, until someone, somewhere at sometime finds evidence that other footsteps were once heard. It's then that the light goes on; it's then that we have a chance to realize that life does not begin and end with us. (May 24, 1988)

A bridge too far, perhaps?

If you were celebrating your 30th birthday, two important points might come to mind: (1) You are no longer 29 but are beginning the "mature" 30s. Time to become part of the establishment. (2) Before you know it, you will be 39 and will never acknowledge another birthday.

The Tappan Zee Bridge may not be a person – although many a harried commuter has cursed it more than any human – but on its 30th birthday it is established. As for reaching age 39, that it will, but the question is will it – and Rockland – survive to see 40 and beyond?

I am among those countyites who can add B.B. (Before Bridge) to their names. I remember the Nyack to Tarrytown ferry. I recall the South Nyack downtown that no longer exists. I built a hut on land now occupied by the Thruway toll exchange at Spring Valley, and I still reel from the thought of long trips to visit my great-grandmother in Brooklyn via Route 9W and the George Washington Bridge.

The Tappan Zee Bridge, the Thruway that made it necessary and the Palisades Interstate Parkway brought great changes to Rockland, some positive, some negative. I have no quarrel with change, but I do dispute the methods by which this county has grown.

Change was inevitable, and we would have had a Hudson River crossing – most probably a tunnel from Alpine to Yonkers – in the '40s had World War II not occurred. The enormous demand for housing following the war, Rockland's suburban location, the increasing reliance on the automobile and the desire of this nation's military leaders to construct a military road network patterned after Germany's autobahn all gave what little push was still necessary to build the Thruway.

However, despite these factors, many fought the planned Thruway and T.Z. Bridge. Numerous homes and businesses – more that 50 in South Nyack alone – were bulldozed and moved to allow construction. Opponents also realized a simpler, friendlier time was about to disappear.

On the other hand, unions and merchants applauded the construction, for it brought jobs and increased sales.

Now, 30 years after the bridge opened, merchants are still happy with the shopping traffic the T.Z. brings. But what about the rest of us? We have all paid a price for its construction. Stand just about anywhere in Rockland on a quiet night, and you will hear the drone of traffic on either the Thruway or the Palisades Interstate Parkway. And Rocklanders shell out more for electricity because expensive, low-sulfur oil must be burned under stricter federal air standards required, in part, because the Thruway and PIP bring auto pollution into the county.

The tremendous growth forced by the superhighways and bridge – doubling Rockland's 1960 population of 137,000 – has not been met with enlightened planning. Congested Route 59, the loss of flood plains, illegal bungalow conversions and far too many shopping centers developed at the expense of downtown areas are proof of that.

Yet Rockland has also benefited. There are more jobs today and a vastly improved standard of living. Housing has been provided for many who could not have left New York City without a commuter link. And the county's heritage has been enriched by a mix of varied peoples and cultures.

Still, we could have done better in the post-bridge era, controlling growth to protect wetlands and greenbelts, seeing to the restoration of older housing, providing ancillary road improvements and looking ahead to that time when a new bridge might be needed to relieve congestion.

The latter point is where we are today. The future of Rockland depends as much on a solution to the bridge congestion as it does on enlightened planning for those vacant areas we have left, particularly along the Hudson River.

My feeling is that if federal authorities want to add traffic from the soon-to-be-built I-287 in New Jersey to the Thruway at Suffern, that traffic should cross the Hudson elsewhere, perhaps over a bridge at Alpine, with Bergen County the site of any new superhighway. Rockland cannot accommodate another bridge at South Nyack simply because the cost has been too great for the first one.

(January 4, 1986)

TV aerials, flags of wealth

It was once part of the suburban experience. In Spring Valley, at least, if you could not get Sound Radio over to put up an aerial for your new-fangled television set and thus show your neighbors that you had arrived, it was you who went up on the roof.

In the early 1950s, as this county was just beginning to build in an earnest way a new life for itself, almost the first thing to appear on tract-home roofs and other homes was the TV aerial. Most of these were installed by homeowners native to Rockland or at least living here for a time, because those newly arrived from New York City at first tended to use the same "rabbit ears" they had in the boroughs.

That was so, perhaps, since TV aerials usually do not do much good there given the large number of high buildings and no place to put the antennas.

In time, even these new Rocklanders would learn that you could not get good reception on Channels 2-13, the only ones available, unless you had a real aerial, on the roof. That was the only way to capture the signals, then coming mostly from the Empire State Building in Manhattan. People in Piermont and some other parts of Rockland where the radio and TV signals were blocked by mountain ranges had trouble no matter what antenna they bought.

If you wanted a roof aerial for your 10-inch or 13-inch set, some with "bubble" magnifiers to enlarge the small picture, you usually called such TV/radio repair places as Sound Radio on Lawrence Street in Spring Valley. They would come to your home, put a ladder against the two-story Cape Cod roof and install a very simple affair, which sometimes required relatively complex wiring.

The antenna would have two elements, one for Channels 2, 4, 5, and the other for Channels 7, 9, 11, 13. You had two wires leading from the aerial to the back of your set and a "knife switch" that had to be thrown to get the best reception for your channel.

No TV remotes, either, so you tended to stay with one channel for a time (somehow that was more satisfying than the "surfing" we now do from the ease of our armchairs).

If you could not afford Sound Radio or were one of the growing number of do-it-yourselfers, you ordered an antenna from Allied Radio or Montgomery Ward or Sears (few stores sold them; you had to use mail order). When it finally came by Railway Express, you enlisted the aid of adults and children to figure out how to put the antenna together.

Then you hauled the various parts to the roof and put it up, hoping you would not fall off. Thereafter began the hilarious orientation process, pointing the aerial toward Gotham, the great unknown to the south, southeast.

You would set up a team of people, including your children, friends and neighbors, to relay shouts of "move it to the left" or "to the right" until you heard from the fellow at the end of the line watching the TV: "That's it!" And you hoped the reception would hold.

Actually, the reception was pretty good. It held for years. The aerial that Sound Radio put up on my parent's 1953 Hillcrest home, later modified by me in 1959, is still on that roof, as is the one the family installed together in 1951 at my grandparent's old home on Tenure Avenue in Spring Valley.

At one time there was a sea of TV aerials throughout Rockland, increasingly more complex in design in an effort to better attract VHF and then UHF channels.

There was more metal on the rooftops than in the Earth's minerals, it seemed. Cable TV put an end to all that, improved reception (after a few years of especially bad signals in Rockland, when the main, non-cable broadcasting antennas were moved to the World Trade Center) and brought us monthly bills.

Thus came to a close a bonding ritual, a barn-raising of sorts among homeowners, their families, neighbors and friends marking Rockland suburbia in the 1950s.

(Dec. 26, 2000)

Section Three
Rockland History

Prayers said in Orangeburg

No one will ever know how many prayers were said in Orangeburg.

No one will ever know how many scared, young men thought of mothers, fathers and wives as they lay in bunks at Camp Shanks, ready to ship out for D-Day and the rest of the action in the European Theatre more than 50 years ago.

Only the individual soldier who fought in that war, following the war to end all world wars, only the mother, father, wife or other loved one of a military person knows what placing oneself in harm's way does to your heart, your mind, your very being for the rest of your life, should you keep your life.

Think of the ranks of soldiers who passed through Shanks, the largest East Coast Army embarkation port, on their way to death, injury, lifelong suffering and never-to-be-forgotten memories, but who also went with the gratitude and pride of a nation convinced that this was the only way to meet advancing Nazism, fascism and Japanese military expansion.

Now we, this nation and its former soldiers, are long friends of our former enemies. Forgiving and generous as Americans are, we helped rebuild their economies, established democracies and now drive Japanese and German cars and use their products. If a soldier went off to war from America in World War II to preserve a nation and the world, he and she also went to extend opportunity to even our former foes.

War should never be the means to better ourselves. Countries' energies are more efficiently and humanely directed at their own internal problems while also helping others in every way they can. But this war, World War II, was one that had a long birth, from the nationalism of the 1800s through the entangling alliances of the pre-Great War years, through the failures of Versailles and rejection of President Woodrow Wilson's peace plan, and through the hatreds and expansionism of Hitler, Mussolini and Tojo. After all that, there came a time when there was no peaceful way to avoid this long-simmering, then boiling, calamity, and the world knew it.

But the ordinary soldier, lying in a bunk at Shanks, did not think of 1870s nationalism. He was a fellow pulled from the farm, just out of school, from a factory (if he had a job in the Great Depression). Here were millions of ordinary Joes who had sweethearts and wives and family, who wanted to live ordinary lives. All that was interrupted for the cause, and to a man they simply wanted to get the job over with and, if it were granted, make it back to move on with life.

Camp Shanks is long gone now, bulldozed over and replanted with suburban tract homes where other generations of ordinary Americans *do* live their dreams. Maybe once in a while, on a misty, quiet night, one of these Rockland suburbanites, in half-sleep, hears jukebox '40s music wafting from a wooden barracks, sees a bunch of fellows in khaki playing cards and senses the fears of a young soldier soon to be on a ship, then at an English port, then on a French beach, all for the unfolding and love of life.

If so, I hope he says yet another prayer in Orangeburg, for all those who passed through Shanks.

(May 17, 1994)

Walking on the 'Boulevard'

You never needed a clock on a summer's night in old Spring Valley. At 7 p.m., almost to the minute, after dinner was eaten and the kids sent out to play with friends, the men and women – but mostly women – would gather for a walk on the "Boulevard."

The Boulevard was the one-mile stretch from Spring Valley to Hillcrest, from the downtown to the Hillcrest Hotel. It was more than a sidewalk. It was a public square, where men discussed politics and women their homes, children and husbands. It was a decision ground, where futures were charted and dreams were verbalized, where mothers talked of lawyers and doctors-to-be. And it was Rockland County's version of the symbolism of Ellis Island and the Statue of Liberty – the walk was appreciated for the freedom to talk and associate.

Many persons of the Jewish faith took the summer walk along the Boulevard, some just months away from pogroms and ghetto poverty. Others were second-generation Americans, whose sense of family and ethnic history kept alive the stories and discrimination and the hope a new nation offered.

As a young child, riding on my bike to the North Main Street School playground, I would see – and hear – the Boulevard walkers, women clad in fur wraps (you had to have something to *show*), talking to friends and calling to others on hotel porches along the way. Being something of a sidelines listener myself, this gentile would cock an ear as walkers extolled or chastised their children, or talked about neighbors or berated working husbands who failed to take the weekend train to Spring Valley.

In the 1950s, the time of my recollection, the village still had many summer resort hotels and bungalows – Bader's, Rubenfeld's, Weissman's, Bauman's, Singer's, Ortner's, to name a few. Spring Valley's population would swell from 6,000 to triple that for the summer months as city dwellers escaped the heat and sought old friends in the best resort outside the Catskills. The village economy was also tied deeply to this seasonal influx.

In time, with the opening of the Tappan Zee Bridge and the Thruway and Palisades Interstate Parkway, many of the summer people – or at least their children – became permanent residents of Rockland. The bungalows gave way to housing developments and, unfortunately in some cases, substandard housing. Change came quickly for Spring Valley and some of its officials and residents were not prepared to meet the challenges.

What should have been an orderly transition of growth from a summer resort to a stable, full-time community of mixed economic levels became, instead, a rapid move to a village beset with more than its share of problems. Lack of planning, the profit motive, new shopping malls, absentee landlords and plain bad luck thrust Spring Valley into an age that no one was prepared to handle.

It's only now – in the 1980s – that the village is showing signs of improvement, of securing a decent life for all its people. As a native Spring Valleyite, I wish it more than luck. It has many good people.

In its age, the Spring Valley of bungalows defined a people particularly determined to succeed, a people who sought better lives for their children, who enjoyed the company of friends and neighbors, who took a walk on hot summer nights on the Boulevard to reaffirm and articulate both their gratefulness for a land and village of opportunity and their determination that the children should do even better.

(June 28, 1986)

A land of past, present

Caught in the Ramapo Mountains' hollow that the Ice Age brought to Rockland, this hamlet of Viola, once of cornfields and orchards and now of homes and a community college, still erupts with beauty in spring and crispness in the fall.

Decades ago, when the county had its almshouse here, in what is now the administration building at Rockland Community College, residents would await their end by watching the farmers toil as they themselves had for so many years.

On any a day, the farmer's cart would take someone on his final journey to the cemetery beyond the cornfield. Summer days were spent sitting under the large oaks and maples on the almshouse grounds, and winters were endured as well as old age allowed.

Years later, in 1959 when RCC was born, students, too, would watch final journeys and farmers in the fields and shiver through the cold days in the shadow of the Ramapos. As elsewhere, the young and old found common ground in Viola.

In the fall, then and now, the old trees would produce an abundance of leaves of all colors, leaving huge limbs exposed like a ship's mast and rigging without a sail, in port for the seasons, but sure to dress for another fine day. In autumn, the air in Viola is unusually crisp, a combination of the fallen foliage and the native winds.

On Viola Road, where a post office once stood, the remains of a thousand apple trees still nurture the soil of development homes. Gone forever is the taste peculiar to fruit bred of this soil, graced by a special wind, hardened by stiff and chilly nights.

On College Road hundreds of cars pass daily to and from RCC and points north and south. Realignment has removed the country lane turns from parts of the road in favor of parkway-like approaches meant for a faster-paced era. The college itself bustles with activity day into night, testimony to Rockland's growth and to an institution.

Beyond the hamlet center, the roads fan out as in times past, some with woods intact and old homes still standing. Take a walk here in the early morning or in twilight and you will feel as though life is no different than in the last century. There are places to hide in Viola, even now.

Viola is not a village, not a town, not even recognized on most maps. It has no post office recognition. Yet it has a spirit, and that gives it its identity. As with the apple orchards of other times, what now exists in Viola cannot fail to be influenced by conditions – feelings, the climate, the unknown – in this hollow by the Ramapo Mountains.
(September 24, 1988)

Grassy Point, in half-fog

One of the best times to walk Grassy Point Road is during a light storm, with the wind blowing a mix of surf and sand off the Hudson River and shore. It is in the subdued light and fog that this area's sand hills, with their characteristic grass, show best.

Once, in a quieter Rockland, before the hurricanes of 1938 and the early 1950s and before the PCBs polluted the Hudson, Grassy Point offered an especially nice beach that reached out straight enough for a large boat landing. (The first steamboat landing was about 1830.) For many years, because of the depth of water at this spot, Grassy Point was the stopping place for steamers passing up and down the river.

In time, clay pits would be developed, shanties built and brick kilns established for the famous North Rockland industry of the 1800s and earlier 1900s. This did much to lessen the flavor of the riverfront at Grassy Point, especially when great clouds of brick dust covered what was left of the grass and the magnificent oaks and chestnut trees upland from the river.

When the industry declined, time returned the sands and grass, and a beauty once hidden was again revealed.

In the 1950s, when the Tappan Zee Bridge pier supports were being built in the area, Rockland drivers would take Routes 202, 59 and 9W from all parts of the county to watch the work. They might stop at the small store, whose name now escapes my mind, near the port side of the beach and buy a large double-dip ice cream cone for 10 cents. They could take a walk along the beach and glance across the Hudson at land not yet developed for a nuclear power plant. And they might stop and fish in the small pools up from the river.

Also in that decade, and again in the 1960s, visitors could see the terrible damage nature can do in one of its storms. Flooding has always been a curse along Grassy Point Road despite concrete barriers and other attempts to contain water that knows no restraint.

Yet certain people have always wanted to live in Grassy Point, perhaps because they have been and are part sea captain, part landlubber. There is the mix of two worlds here and the conveniences and inconveniences of both. At night, when the visitors have left and the homestead lights cast a glow in streaks on the river, the residents have their quiet world to themselves once again. It's a world that looks out on a frontier of sorts, as the Hudson has always been.

There may be heavy traffic on Route 59, there may be loud parties in the suburbs, there may be construction everywhere, but at Grassy Point, the native can light his sea lantern if he wants to, swing it from the front porch and there sit and enjoy what long has been a windward quality of life. (November 26, 1988)

Tappan, cradle of history

Once the county seat of Orange, Tappan, this busy political crossroads of early America, proved fertile ground where the ideas of freedom, Revolutionary War plans and judgment for spying were uttered in the King's English but on the lips of free men.

Yet while history has been made in Tappan by the Orangetown Resolutions, which stated a people's intent to be free; by George Washington's headquarters and all its war councils; and by the hanging in 1780 of 30-year-old British Maj. John André for spying for his nation – while all this and more history has passed through Tappan proper, major commercial life and attendant growth have passed it by.

Originally, Tappan referred to all the land within the huge Orangetown patent, just as Paramus was formerly the name of all the country from Sneden's Landing to the Ramapo River. Tappan Landing was the present Piermont and Tappan Slote was Sparkill. The village center of Tappan was the first organized hamlet in the area from Newburgh to the New Jersey border.

What promise there was in this region, what great thoughts of commerce, especially since it was the county seat. Yet for reasons largely uncertain, it has been Tappan's destiny to be largely forgotten in its post-Revolutionary War history.

The building of the Erie Railroad in the 1840s left the hamlet to the south, and the opening of the Northern Railroad in 1857-59 passed it by to the east. Eventually, the New York, West Shore and Buffalo Railroad came through the hamlet, but even that run, which now exists only as a well-used freight line, did nothing for Tappan but continue its fate as a way stop on the road of history.

If you believe in ghosts and retribution of the dead, you might think Maj. André's spirit has prevented Tappan's material growth and large commercial success. No matter what the reason, though, you'll get no argument about the result from present residents of the hamlet center. They're happy with quiet, charming Tappan.

If it were the county seat, it would be bustling like New City. There would be more strip shopping, more homes, more traffic, big buildings and a downtown atmosphere. That's not for Tappan. It's enough that its people can walk the green from the Manse to the Old Reformed Church, or stroll past the restored '76 House, look in the small shops that offer a distinct colonial flavor, sit in the park dedicated to the labors of those residents who recognize the hamlet's unique history, and spend hours in the library enjoying books written years before and read and felt by generations long gone.

Tappan today is busier than the Tappan of 1694, when the first school was formed under the good Dutchman Hermanus Van Huysen. The hamlet is modern, for sure. It has housing developments, shopping centers and traffic.

Yet, the history that began in that schoolhouse, the events that unfolded in the hamlet proper, still embrace Tappan as if they were together a cloak that has yet to be fully unbuttoned. You cannot help but feel that Tappan's story is not complete, but, rather, on hold.

(July10, 1990)

Roots in Suffern's success

Choose a relatively cool late summer night, walk along Lafayette Avenue in Suffern and stop to look up and about. You will see the same distant hills that drew John Suffern in September 1763 from Antrim, Ireland.

When he began his general store near the intersection of what is now Routes 59 and 202, he ushered in a thriving commercial life for this village, which soon would become prominent on the Nyack Turnpike. All manner of goods would eventually be collected at Suffern, some sold, but many sent down to the flat-bottomed boats at Nyack and to export.

In time, Suffern found New Antrim, as the village was then called, a suitable place to develop a grist mill, a forge and a woolen factory on the Mahwah River. With the opening of the Erie Railroad in 1841, New Antrim took the name of Suffern in John's honor. Today, Suffern is still a vital commercial center, although its downtown shopping heyday was in the 1950s, when it vied with Nyack for the best stores. Indeed, some businesses operated two stores, one in Suffern and one in Nyack. And for many years, the Lafayette Theatre was one of the major places Rockland youngsters chose to spend a Saturday afternoon.

Once, when the Main Line/Port Jervis Line ran a train up the Southern Tier, Suffernites and other Rocklanders could take a fine Sunday ride, passing through numerous small, upstate towns. Now the line is commuter and freight, and the village itself is host daily to many a New York City-bound traveler.

Suffern, like Spring Valley, long has had a large parking lot behind the downtown stores, a place where kids wait as mom and dad shop. At one time there were a few old cars and trucks there, too, and an ancient bus. For the price of using one's imagination, the wait was passed quickly and in great fun as the youngsters played in these vehicles.

In spring, when the trees are beginning to blossom, a walk along Washington Avenue, past the magnificent Sacred Heart Church, the old school that is now Village Hall, and up to the Suffern Free Library is a walk in the essence of America. Here you see fine, old, well-kept homes, tree-lined streets and slate sidewalks. It is a most satisfying sight.

Green's "History of Rockland County" tells us that the first store in what is now the present Village of Suffern was built in 1842 by George W. Suffern. In 1884, Suffern contained 20 stores, 90 homes, two hotels and 600 people. (January 20, 1990)

Pomona, in the evening

There are nights, about this time of year, when the day's warm breath lingers over the fields of Pomona. You can't quite feel the heat's afterglow, but you can smell and taste the woodsy nectar so peculiar to this valley off the Ramapo Mountains.

I fell in love with Pomona in her rural days, before Pomona Road ran – as it does today – as a wide route from the office buildings at Route 45 to the developments on Route 306. Then, you rode hairpin turns from Concklin's orchards to the Pomona Country Club to Lime Kiln, passing an old farmhouse here and a bungalow there.

I had friends in Pomona then – the Galbreaths, Prescotts, Hurleys, Madawicks – each suited to the country character of Pomona in his or her way. Some were staunch, independent woodsmen cast from the pioneer mold, others were from old-line families watching the ever-sure changing of the guard.

And some were artists whose sensitivity matched the soft fields at the Country Club (not really a "country club," but an area of private homes).

My seasons were short but varied and plentiful in this countrified region. I worked at a day camp for two years; I was caught by a winter storm one time and stayed the night at a friend's house in a delicious old featherbed; and for two seasons I felt the pangs of young romance.

Those were times of trial by growing up, of making mistakes and not knowing it, of lost opportunity but also of gathering strength.

I'm convinced that we all pass through moments in our lives as if we were not there at all. We feel things, yes, and we can recall particular moments, but, years later, when we look back from a new perspective, we see just bits and pieces of the individual we are now.

Would if we could, we might return and relive the original moment, only better this time.

Pomona has changed, as does everything. It has a different sort of beauty today, one which others will surely recall years from now as I do the Pomona of my past.

Yet the village of today has in common with the hamlet of yesterday a common characteristic: the smell of the woods and fields on a warm evening. It has not changed, beckoning as it still does, like a mysterious woman whose perfume you cannot forget.

(May 20, 1986)

Between two worlds

It is raining as I write this in West Nyack at 6:41 a.m. on a Saturday, and I am caught between two worlds. One, to the south, looking out the office window, is Route 59, a divided highway that old Rocklanders thought was an interstate when it was built about the time the big E.G. Korvette shopping center came to Nanuet in the 1950s.

Rockland was already firmly on the map then as spurting suburbia, and shopping centers were also the rage, especially for a county that had a "Thruway" and a bridge across the Hudson River, both spanking new. Soon to be on board was the Palisades Interstate Parkway, which most Rocklanders of the later 1950s saw as a route for weekend New York City tourists bent for Bear Mountain, but during the week they claimed it for their own, as another way to get here and there, a private highway.

Actually, weekday traffic north of New City was so light that parents taught their children how to drive on the PIP.

So, here I am, in October 2005, looking at post-1955 Rockland, hearing the vehicles whiz by on "new" Route 59, even at this early hour, even on a lazy Saturday. Even in the rain that used to limit traffic. The view south out of the window at the new Journal News offices is typical Rockland. Soon, Route 59 will be abuzz with all the regular irregulars: traffic zoomers, those afflicted with "fingeritis," who fail to signal, the nut jobs who race up to the light at Crosfield Avenue and then screech to a halt, saving perhaps one minute total on the run to the shopping centers west on 59.

Ah, another day dawns and rises and unfolds in Rockland. Ho hum.

But I said I was caught between two worlds, which literally I am as a pre-Tappan Zee Bridge countyite and one who endures, as many of you do, too much growth.

The other world this morning, this rainy day, is what is for me and such fellow oldtimers as Wally Ackerson, now a West Nyacker, the "real" Route 59, for a short time in the late 1950s and early 1960s named Old Route 59 and then West Nyack Road. It was retired as a state highway when the "bigger and better" divided four-laner was built from Nanuet's Four Corners to the swamp at West Nyack.

Once, old 59 was, in my youth and Wally's, too, a two-lane concrete highway, part of the Old Nyack Turnpike, which connected the Four Corners in Nanuet and Spring Valley, Monsey, Tallman/Airmont and Suffern with what was east, Nyack.

When we were kids, we took what was almost never a busy road to the movies in the grand old theater on Broadway in Nyack, or to watch the ferry depart for Tarrytown, just as Rockland veterans affairs director Jerry Donnellan did as a Nyacker.

Your parents may have taken this road to have you born at Nyack Hospital, as John Romaine did in October 1943 when his wife Marie went into awfully quick labor, and he somehow made it all the way to Nyack from Church Street, Spring Valley, a five-mile trip, in four or so minutes. His daughter Lucille (Wally's wife) is proof that her father and the road held up well.

My father walked this old state road all the way home to Spring Valley from the Nyack ferry landing in the late 1930s after trying to join the Navy. He was rejected for (ironically) bad feet, but the Marines took him anyway.

My first car broke down on old Route 59 in October 1960, and I hoofed it home to the Valley. Fall was always beautiful on this now-retired section of 59, and the steep, curved hill up from the Clarksville Inn gave you time to enjoy it all. If it were raining, the added glisten rendered artist's varnish to the scene.

Now, in our new office, I can look to the left, south, for the new, and to the right, north for the old. Having both worlds is a bit of OK, since despite my crabiness, lots of things are fun in 2005. But the magnet truly points north. Always.

(October 25, 2005)

Nanuet, a hub, crossroads

Most now mark the hamlet of Nanuet by the presence of a shopping mall and other stores, or by Routes 59 and 304, or by the commuter parking lots for the Pascack Valley Line. Nanuet is a Rockland crossroads, and many of us pass through it at least once a week.

This image of Nanuet has rung true since 1856, when the hamlet's name was changed from Clarkstown to Nanuet (after an Indian chief). From that time on, the railroad and Nanuet's central location on the Nyack Turnpike and Middletown Road fostered development. A hotel, tavern and grocery store were built to serve travelers and others who came to buy agricultural equipment, lumber and coal from the Hutton brothers.

For years, most of the activity centered on the downtown, around the Highview School or near coal yards. Clarkstown police also had its headquarters here, if you can call a room a police station. In pre-'60s times, Rocklanders would come to the hamlet to buy pizza pie (no one called it just pizza then) from the Nanuet Hotel and then, also, from the Nanuet Restaurant (as people still do today). There was a small barbershop where kids got a monthly haircut, a part-time bakery known for its lemon meringue pies and enough marshland, streams and light woods where the Nanuet Mall now sits to keep a youngster busy all day chasing frogs and collecting cattails.

A walk to school meant a hike up Orchard to the Highview building, where lunch was always followed by the PTA-sponsored candy cart, the most popular part of the meal. The community was too small for its own high school and eighth-grade graduates went to Nyack, Pearl River or Spring Valley high schools. And a sense of community pervaded, as when the Lutheran church burned down and the Jewish temple allowed worshippers to use its facilities for a year until the church rebuilt in New City.

In those years, as in the present, the Pascack Valley Line carried commuters to Hoboken, but it also brought coal and lumber to the great yards behind what are now stores and the post office. Huge machinery would take the coal from railroad cars daily and youngsters would walk along the tracks and yard to pick up what they could for use in home stoves.

Nanuet proper is now surrounded by homes and satellite businesses, growing out from the hub of commerce and living that the hamlet has always been. If the average longtime Rocklander had a penny for every day he passed through Nanuet, he would be rich.

(October 29, 1988)

Holiday greetings to 'Town'

It's holiday time, with Hanukkah just past and Christmas heading our way, and writing cards always reminds me of an old small-town Post Office tradition that would never fly today.

It was too Pony Express, I guess. Too small town, literally. But, oh so Currier & Ives or Norman Rockwell.

When I was younger, growing up in Spring Valley and beginning to send out a few holiday cards on my own, using my father's stamps and my mother's cards, I learned an old trick.

It was Helen Rouy's instruction, actually. She was my teacher in the third grade at the old South Main Street School and her sister, Amy, taught me English in the 10th grade at Spring Valley High.

The sisters, both unmarried, lived in a grand old family house on Ridge Street, with an old attic full of wind-up Victrolas, some of which they later gave to John Romaine, a TV/radio expert who was friends with the sisters.

Both Rouys were excellent teachers, especially in writing instruction, and their classes seemed to have the least behavioral problems. Maybe that was because they genuinely liked their students and got them interested in all manner of subjects, ranging from "The Wizard of Oz" to local matters.

Local matters. The Rouys would send out cards at holiday time, of course, and Helen would have us write some in class. She and Helen Still, our wonderful fourth-grade teacher, would bring in old cards not used, some decades old and beautifully done, and place them on the chalkboard ledge for us to take and send ourselves.

We would thus learn the art of writing a short message on a card and then correctly addressing the envelope.

When it came to sending to our friends in Spring Valley, long before the Zip Code days when it would simply become a number (10977), we were told to write something like: Joel Levenson, John Street, Town.

"Town?" Yes, Town. The Valley Post Office, staffed by locals, knew that Town meant anywhere in the Spring Valley Postal District, which included the village, Hillcrest, part of Nanuet, etc.

We were assured that we did not have to write "Spring Valley, N.Y."

There was a certain warmth in that knowledge, especially at holiday time when cookies, decorations and family gatherings, hopefully under a canopy of snow, would bring warmth by nature.

Using "Town" on the envelope was like belonging to a special, private club or group; you came from Town and your friends did, too.

Of course, in other towns, they could also write to "Town" and be equally assured of a letter's arrival, with the post being delivered twice a day during holidays and also on Sunday.

But for Spring Valleyites, our own use of "Town" was quite special, as instructed by the Rouy sisters.

(Dec. 10, 2002)

Weeping in Pearl River

They are weeping in Pearl River.

Weeping for New York City's Bravest and Finest, apparently lost in the rubble and horror and smoke of the World Trade Center disaster.

They are weeping elsewhere in Rockland, surely, for civilians and city workers alike, but it is Pearl River and all of Orangetown where so many of the Bravest and Finest live.

Some neighborhoods are almost an extension of the city, and firefighters and police officers living there have taken the jobs of fathers, grandfathers, great-grandfathers.

This is another Rockland, set apart from the country and historic days, and distinct from the regular post-war suburbia of New City or the ethnically diverse neighborhoods of Spring Valley and Haverstraw.

In that, there is as much heritage, distinction and pride as in any section of this geographically small county so close to New York City.

Indeed, it is the physical closeness that makes Pearl River, particularly, so attractive to city workers.

When the Palisades Interstate Parkway partially opened in 1955, Orangetown was the first accessible area, 16 miles from the George Washington Bridge.

Firefighters and police officers, seeking a country life for their families and unable by law to live in closer New Jersey, flocked to the relatively affordable housing in Rockland.

And they formed a community. It is not the usual suburbia.

Yes, there are the bi-levels; the block parties; the hustle and bustle of car pools and family activity.

But there is also the "Brotherhood."

The Brotherhood of deep concern and respect for each officer, active or retired, and son or daughter or father or grandchild of that officer.

You might just as well be in the firehouse or the police precinct station house on many streets of Pearl River.

These people stick together, and when one suffers, all do, fueled by the deep sense of mourning that the Irish (and so many of these officers are of that heritage) instinctively carry in their souls and hearts.

Rockland, Pearl River, do not yet know how many of their New York City Bravest and Finest will be counted on the honor roll of the dead. That may take weeks, and the toll may be high.

But already the darkness of grief has descended, and with that sweep of fate are also seen angels of mercy and comfort.

It is the mutual-aid system of the Brotherhood of firefighters and police officers that has eased into the grief, separating the dark from hope and resurrection and thanks for sacrifice.

The bagpipes will be playing a long time in Pearl River and in Rockland.

The Masses will be many. There will be a lifetime of sorrowful memory.

But already there has begun a healing, thanks be to God, by the goodness of the Brotherhood.

(Sept. 14, 2001)

'B-matter' blue-plate special

Time: 4 a.m. Place: The old Hogan's Diner on Route 59, West Nyack, long before the Palisades Center Mall was built. This was the railroad-style restaurant, circa 1966, not the big diner the Hogans later trucked in from the factory.

I'm pulling the night shift as a Journal News photographer, and I've been to one of the very long Stony Point Planning Board meetings that sometimes took us to 1 a.m. I've been back to the downtown Nyack newspaper offices, processed my film and printed my photographs. Now, I'm headed home, to get up in a few hours to go to college. (I was working and going to college in the later '60s because I flubbed the chance to do just school a few years before.)

I'm hungry, and I'm at the diner counter, just in front of the cook, who's at the grill. This is the seat of great importance at the old-style diner, the ones that looked like trolleys and did not have the grill out back, out of view.

You saw your food being cooked, and you also got great smells as an appetizer. You were set up for a feast by the early-morning mix of a steaming pile of home fries and onions, some bacon cooking for a customer, and then maybe your grilled cheese on the grill, after one of the Hogans or their itinerant cooks took processed American from the refrigerator next to the grill, put a slab of butter on the fry space and threw your sandwich near that delicious mix.

And the tab was fine, too, with grilled cheese, French fries and a Coke or coffee at $1.25.

But you also got a goodly dose of what we in newspapers call "b-matter," the background or biography fill for any particular story. In this instance, in all the trips to old Hogan's, or to any other diner in the wee hours, we got b-matter for life.

The counter seat, in front of the grill man, brought your ears close to talk about politics or someone's troubles, or juicy gossip. You could hear the people down a stool or two, hunched over coffee, a cigarette in hand, discussing this or that, with one guy usually in a state of fervor and the other quietly listening.

So, I'm at the counter, on the stool, in front of the cook, and I'm young (24 years old) and eager and fascinated by any slice of life that hits the slab each day (or night). I file away the b-matter for use in a story, for amusement, for reaffirmation that we are all characters

Being in those old diners was like reading a book a night, tapping into what seemed like ordinary characters, but who really were either intellectual beyond belief, or wrapped up in deep political intrigue or up to their waist in this social situation or that.

And all heard under the unwritten but firm rule of those old diners: anonymity. I heard a lot there, and, yes, I used some of that in newspaper stories or for tips to the city desk, but mostly I kept the confidence of these largely anonymous souls.

The grill man was perhaps the most "unseen" fellow, though he was also the most visible. If he were one of the Hogans, like the late ex-prize fighter Billy, you knew him and maybe he'd ask you a question or two (though Billy wasn't all that talkative).

But if the cook were the itinerant type, the fellow who hopped from diner to diner all along the Eastern Seaboard, he largely kept quiet, efficiently tending to the grill, grabbing a cigarette, which he kept at the counter's edge with ash-defying gravity, sometimes staring off into space (looking for the next job or back at some opportunity lost, perhaps), while he leaned against the bread drawer, half a once-white apron wrapped around his waist.

Yes, b-matter. It still exists in diners, but it's harder to find now that the cook is in the back, now that the diner is so huge and now that the counter stools are rarely used.

(Oct. 24, 2000)

A night on High Tor

The sun was nearing the end of its day's work when the two of us began to climb up High Tor. Central Highway was not yet complete, so the easiest way was the approach from the High Tor Vineyards. It was the start of an evening that would prove anything but easy.

I knew this particular way up the Haverstraw mountain because I had taken it many times with friends and by myself. You drove up the winding, private lane leading off South Mountain Road to the vineyards, parked your car and approached High Tor from the back. It was a long climb, about an hour, and involved lumbering over some steep, almost vertical rocks – the famous trap rock of the Palisades.

Most of the climb, however, was simple, because you were able to follow a thick cable leading directly to the Tor from the vineyard area. Supplying power to an aircraft beacon atop the mountain, the cable was mostly visible as it stretched over rocks and alongside streams. That night the cable would prove to be of some added value.

My companion and I jumped out of the Volkswagen at about 6:30 that hot, sticky August evening, intending to make a quick run up the mountain and then come right back. I thought it was a good place for a date because I enjoyed the quiet of the woods and sitting atop High Tor was the summit of that feeling, surrounded as you are by nothing but the whistling wind. If my date did not like the idea of hiking up the Tor, I wasn't yet aware of that.

The two of us found the cable and followed it across the several streams that lie just before what was in the early '60s a great open field. At the other side you began the ever-more steep ascent. Before we knew it, we were scaling the trap rock with the High Tor beacon in the distance. Soon we were actually on the mountain, I on the edge looking down at Haverstraw Bay, she 10 yards or so away, studying Low Tor to the north.

We had enjoyed the climb, which we had made before. Everything had gone smoothly, but going down would prove a different story. By the time we reached the Tor, the sun was just raising its eyebrow at us, bidding good night and leaving us bathing in an initially strong but diminishing radiance. The rocks still gave off the summer's heat, but the wind, no longer warmed by the sun, provided contrast. Not only did we have our quiet, but we felt somewhat majestic sitting atop all of Rockland, away from the concerns of life "down there."

It was as if the sun was going to sleep for the night and had tipped his hat to us, his night watchmen.

We enjoyed the beauty for a long time, longer that we had intended, until it was just about pitch dark. The sun has a way of playing tricks on you, lulling you into the false security of its full light so that you trust its afterglow for too long. We were about to pay a price for that.

How to get down, we wondered, not just a little frightened. High Tor is surrounded by much wooded area and it's possible to get lost very quickly, even in daylight. We decided to find the beacon cable and follow that, which worked for a time only. And then we were lost.

What followed – for almost three hours – was a meandering run, sometimes in circles, through the High Tor and Low Tor woods, our legs scratched by briar bushes, our feet wet from sudden drops into streams, our wind lost to exhaustion only to return, fueled by fear and adrenalin.

Eventually, we found the cable again and that proved to be the way out. We ended up in the rear of the vineyard, which I came upon with suddenness when my head hit the tailpipe of a white Jaguar owned by vineyard operator Everett Crosby. I had backed into a clearing that suddenly dropped five feet, and we were walking below the car when my head hit it, a pain most welcome.

In time we would return to the Tor again, but in daylight. And while the relationship would not prove as endurable as the mountain, I sometimes think back to the test High Tor gave us that night. For we had taken of its beauty, had paid a price for it, but had also emerged intact, the two of us at least a good team for mountain climbing and the endurance of danger.
(April 24, 1983)

Perruna's a 'clubhouse'

If you were a youth in his or her late teens who happened by Spring Valley's Main Street in the 1950s, you probably ended up at Perruna's Restaurant.

That is, if you could get in. This family restaurant by day and young people's mecca by Friday and Saturday night had lines that ran all the way up and down Main Street. Youth waited a long time in the cold, rain and snow.

And it was worth it. The pizza was the best thin crust this writer has ever eaten; the atmosphere was convivial, with Valleyites of various high school classes at this table or that; and you met many new people.

Yes, there was drinking at Perruna's, especially with the alcohol age lower in New York than in neighboring New Jersey, but that wasn't all there was to it, by far. There was companionship, getting together with your buddies.

Besides, Vic Perruna and Joe Shelly, the proprietors, ran a clean place, and they had rules. No rude, loud behavior; no fights; behave yourself. Or you got bounced by Vic, Joe or by Frank Jacaruso and, later, George D'Loughy, the bartenders.

It was coming of age for many a young Valleyite and others to go to Perruna's, second only to being at the Tigers Den, the Friday and Saturday night school-sponsored meeting place built by community support and vocational students in the 1940s just off Memorial Park.

Actually, many teens would go to both places on any given Friday or Saturday night. If you had some money, you might stay longer at Perruna's.

By day and on other nights, Perruna's was a family eating place, a haven for the business lunch crowd or a special-occasion spot to visit.

Many a young relationship began (and ended) in Perruna's; many a goodbye was said, but also many a hello. Lifelong friendships were forged.

And you got much practice hearing people above the din, since the noise level was enough to drive all the birds from a park. You also could not move your chair too far because the tables were over-occupied, and there was little floor space.

Coming of age anywhere always involves a "clubhouse." Perruna's offered us the keys to one such place in the Spring Valley of the 1950s. (Oct. 9, 2001)

Along the Ramapo River

Nature may be conspiring to parch our thirst with the worst of the four-year drought so far, hitting us where it hurts as we raise an ever-bigger glass in the modern insatiable appetite.

But take a walk along the Ramapo River, in the Suffern-Hillburn-Sloatsburg region, and despite the fact that it is this water which is disappearing, you can almost forget why we Rocklanders in the year 2003 consume so much.

Walk here, along the banks where the Lenni-Lenapi and descendants of the Ramapough Indians fished, view the native habitat, know and feel the history, and you wonder why you should ever return to society. Indian trails follow streams and brooks, and the portion along the Ramapo was well-trodden.

It is quiet here, nothing stirring, save the scampering small animals and the occasional snake out for water and sunning on the river rocks in an emerging spring.

Look about and you will recall the early American industry and mills of Sloatsburg, and you realize how necessary the water was for power and sustenance.

If a power plant were to built below Torne Mountain, as proposed, you would hardly recognize the river area. Indeed, this section would surely return the walker to modern humankind and what can be the excesses of living.

More power. Bigger cars. Simply cannot do without this or that. Wade in the water, and you can see how smooth it is, washed repeatedly by the rocks that make Rockland famous. Yet the wellfield upon which it stands is lower than ever and could dry up in man's time.

The Ramapo is so many, many thousands of years old, formed by the Glacial Age that gave Rockland its unique features, including a large aquifer. It remained pristine most of that time, giving in to the early industrialization of the 1700s and man's push in the 1800s as Rockland began to build.

The nation's first lengthy rail line, the Erie, came alongside the Ramapo. Then a major U.S. highway, Route 17. Then the Thruway, one of the big interstates of 1950s progress, crossed it.

Then homes were built. And industries closed. And the Ramapo actually settled into a rather quiet life. So quiet, in fact, that it takes a hike along its banks to know the fact. No view from a speeding car on the interstate can tell you that.

It is spring along the Ramapo, and to get there and take a solitary walk, you must deal with the increasingly heavy traffic that multiplies every year, even every month, in Rockland.

Perhaps 10 horn blasts later on the ride from West Nyack, one traffic jam, several close calls from non-signaling motorists and a partial fill at the gas station, you park and leave the car and take the walk. The deeper you get into the land along the Ramapo, especially on a beautiful, 72-degree day, the less willing you are to hike back and return to the car and the traffic.

Somewhere along the Ramapo River, you wonder why, with such beauty, we had to leave it behind in the search for the comforts of "progress."
(April 23, 2002)

Lafayette, the 'cat's pajamas'

The old Lafayette Theatre in Suffern was the cat's pajamas when I was young.

Spring Valley had its own movie house, and that's where most of us went in the 1950s , for 14 cents a seat, later 25 cents. Until it burned after Christmas 1960 ("Village of the Damned" was playing), it was a mecca for kids, teens and adults.

Like most theaters of its day, it gave out dishes and turkeys at holiday time and towels to spur business. And like movie houses in all small downtowns, when you gathered with friends, it was an extension of school assembly time: the same chums up to the same mischief. Only there were no teachers, just slightly older teen-age ushers with ill-fitting jackets, big flashlights and temporary authority, who stared you down and sometimes asked someone to leave.

But they never bothered you when you were enjoying your first movie house "stolen" kiss, which I made sure came my way in the seventh grade with my Hillcrest next-door neighbor.

So, the Valley Theatre was our own house, and it felt comfortable there. You often sat in the same seats. The Lafayette in Suffern, however, was reserved for classier times.

When there was an especially big movie, like "Alice in Wonderland" or "Bambi," my father would run my brother Craig and me the six miles to Suffern and let us off at the Doughboy statue. We would then join a long line of other kids, most of whom we did not recognize. We felt a bit alien, like we were intruding on someone else's space. (After all, the Suffern kids knew this was their movie home.)

The Lafayette was grand, with what we now call Art Deco beauty, though then we kids thought it was just a room taken from a French king's court.

It was larger than the Valley Theatre, and the screen was bigger. The candy was just as expensive as in Spring Valley, but we usually sneaked in our own (there were signs that it was "illegal" to bring in candy to either movie house).

It was always fun when you went to the Lafayette, for getting in the car, leaving Spring Valley and going to Suffern was a rare treat.

Over the years, we would occasionally return to the Lafayette, and when I learned to drive and had just graduated from high school, I saw "Guns of Navarone" with a date from Pomona who told me in advance that she did not approve of stolen kisses in movie theaters. But I had been there, done that, five years before.

Sometime later, sans girlfriend, in the fall of 1961, as I was trying to figure out what to do in life, I went to the Lafayette on my own to see "Splendor in the Grass" with Natalie Wood. It was one of those earlier psychological dramas, well done with Warren Beatty, and I have never forgotten how its solitude matched my own mood of the moment.

In fact, whenever I see a large clock with a fluorescent light ring around it, like the one the Lafayette and other movie houses had, I think of that film and that time, for I usually sat under the clock.

Glad to see that the old Lafayette is coming back to life.
(December 3, 2002).

On the boards at Playhouse

The old Tappan Zee Playhouse on South Broadway in Nyack is again in the news, this time because the village may allow a commercial building, a park or recreation center there. Whatever comes, it will have to share the space with the ghosts of thespians and others.

At one time, I am informed, the grounds were the site of a Native American trading post. A playhouse was built there early in this century, which also served as a silent movie theater. Only the front entry facade and side walls of the structure remain.

Many actors, most now long gone, have been on its old boards through the ages. One time, the late Helen Hayes, the Nyack actress, made a surprise appearance to play a bit of a joke on fellow actors.

If I were to have other lives, one surely would be as an actor. There is enough ham in me to do that, and it's usually the shy people like me who let it all hang out on the stage anyway.

Thespians have a true sense of camaraderie, not unlike that in newspapering; you can be an individual, my most precious right, but also be part of a community.

In my earlier years, as a staff photographer for The Journal News, I usually drew the summer stock assignments at the Playhouse. That was always interesting work, though I rarely had time to appreciate what I was doing.

Al Witt, my old photo boss, was ever piling on the assignments, so I usually had to move quickly to another rendezvous. I also was young and not really impressed by anyone with a name.

One time I was there to get a shot of Gloria Swanson. She had a rental Rolls outside the stage door, and I was beckoned in to her dressing room, which was so small it looked like one-half of a closet. The rows of light bulbs around the mirror were there, and so was the makeup.

The actress sat with great dignity and aplomb for the shot.

Actors always make for a good photo shoot, because they are used to taking direction from cameramen and directors, lighting designers, etc. They know also, by instinct, how to give us their "best side," and we can almost always count on a dramatic pose, or at least one that reveals the character of the moment.

About the only difficult actor I dealt with was the late Sam Levine, who was directing "Three Men on a Horse." I came into the Tappan Zee on a very hot afternoon in the late '60s, interrupted his direction and told Levine what I wanted.

His quick reply, delivered like one of the tough guys he sometimes played in the movies, was "Sonny, nothing is photographed without my complete direction." Well, with five minutes before I had to leave for my next assignment, I growled within but seemed agreeable to him on the outside. That was a frequent tactical move by this photographer, who found that you could get what you wanted simply by saying "yes" and not really doing what was asked, at least not in the same way. It's the "no" that most people don't want to hear.

I let Levine set up the shot, but I took it from my angle, which meant putting one actor in the foreground and others in the rear, for depth, and using only the available stage lighting, for drama.

Many actors passed through the Playhouse in the 1960s, when I was taking photographs, and opening night always made for an exciting scene, with dressed-up people attending, swank cars lined up and the occasionally really famous actor sitting in the audience to applaud a fellow thespian.

In a very real way, the old Indian trading post simply was continued, with actors trading characterization for applause.
(October 17, 2000).

Quiet in Rockland

The quiet was remarkable, and you could spot the sparkle of bygone days, as you can when you catch an older person in a reflective mood and look at his or her face.

It was the early time in Rockland, about 7 a.m. on a Sunday, perhaps the only hour of the only day of the week when the commuterites are not hell-bent for the traffic jam and Gotham and wherever else; and when the hundreds of small school vans are not hopping here and there; and when the great suburban animal that is now this county is not yet awake.

It was the quiet time in Rockland, and for those of us with some memory of, say, four decades ago, and maybe even before the Tappan Zee Bridge and Palisades Interstate Parkway, it was evidence of what lower volume then played into our ears, though we did not think it unusual.

Even in those days, each morning, save the weekends, brought a development bulldozer somewhere, but the roads were still easy to navigate without heavy traffic or impolite drivers; the downtowns still existed for walkers and shoppers; and you could find proof of a simpler, country life by leaving your keys in the car on the street overnight, never even thinking it might be stolen.

Summers then, and this may be partly the amplification of memory, brought sweeter smells, perhaps because the farms were still here, and apple and peach orchards in season have a near-heaven scent if you walk through them on an early morning.

Route 59, then a two-lane road in most sections, was the busy road, joined at times by Routes 9W, 303 and 202, even Route 45. But Route 304 out of New City was just a meandering country path, including the almost rural county Main Street. Where the old Route 304, North Main Street, is now being widened to near Long Island Expressway capacity, there was still the look of the horse parading and training there at Squadron Acres and the existence of nature's flooding plain for the Hackensack River, now so built over.

Rockland was growing then, too, as the bulldozer reminded us each day, but most of us thought there would be enough room for growth, if we thought about the future at all. We never expected it to reach over-capacity or that the planning would be so lacking in vision that our infrastructure would be as overloaded as it is today.

Now, the quiet is hard to find, though I managed to get an earful that recent Sunday morning when it seemed as if it were 1960 or even 1952 Rockland. I half expected that my car would direct me to Tiny's Diner, next to Joe Judge's Windmill bar (a structure shaped like a windmill) on Route 59 in Spring Valley.

There, at Tiny's and later at Joe's, the Rockland quiet took on greater volume, with the discussion of neighbors and friends concentrated in country space. Warm space.

If you had looked at my face that recent Sunday morning, when I rediscovered Rockland's quiet, you would have seen a reflection of that warmth.

Guess I miss it.

(August 8, 2000).

Front porch and daily parade

You know what you don't see much of anymore in Rockland? Porch-sitters, that's what. At one time, beginning with spring and ending in the first days of fall, people would congregate on their front porches along Nyack's Broadway, Haverstraw's Hudson Avenue and Spring Valley's North and South Main streets, and elsewhere in Rockland.

Many of these homes were Victorians, with wide, wraparound porches that offered views on at least two sides of the home. Your grandfather would cover the special porch decking with gray or green paint each season, making it shine. The oil-based paint would give off its characteristic smell each spring, and even if you did not have a porch of your own, walking down the street past the homes would clue you in that a new season had begun.

In the days when communities were smaller, you'd have the regular porch-sitters, usually older folks who were retired. They'd nod to you as you walked past or say hello or keep tabs on you. If you were with someone you shouldn't be or doing something not quite right, the porch-sitter was sure to telegraph the message to your parents pronto.

These porches were also the perfect place to pick up neighborhood gossip and were replaced in succeeding years by such gathering spots as the backyard clothesline, the side yard fence, the community swimming pool, the local garage and the pick-up line at the nursery school.

In times past, the old front porches were gaily decorated for the Fourth of July, offered a respite (coolness and lemonade) for the postman, were the repository for your local newspaper (if the paperboy had good aim) and allowed many to observe the daily parade that was small-town America.

Now, many of these porches are empty. People are too busy, or they sit in screened-in back porches, or on behind-the-house sun decks made of pressure-treated lumber, or they congregate around pools. Today, the daily parade is more often watched from the armchair in front of the TV, and the parade is that of the global community, not the local one.

There's both progress and regress in that. We're learning about other peoples but we're also losing touch with those in our own towns. In their time, the old front porches gave us a window on an important world. (September 25, 1990).

A tree grows in West Nyack

There may be a famous tree growing in Brooklyn, but Rockland has at least one equally significant perennial plant. Considering where it lies, it is a wonder that it has survived. And not only that, it is actually thriving.

I first noticed it when I was biking Sunday, working up a sweat on Route 303 from both the exercise and the heavy traffic. I don't make a habit of biking on major roads but could not avoid a short stretch of 303 in West Nyack since I had to get from old Route 59 to Snake Hill Road. It was at the intersection of the Thruway with 303 and Snake Hill that I saw this tree.

I had just passed under the Thruway overpass and made my way – gingerly – over the Thruway exits and entrances when I spotted something I could not believe: apples. And red ones at that. Big, red, ripe apples.

From a tree that is growing out of a pile of litter probably thrown by a motorist in 1962. Next to the Thruway. In a gully, where water laced with road salt is the winter norm.

Behind the tree are the northbound lanes of the Thruway. Cars zip by. The noise is deafening. The tree even sways a bit from the gush of the traffic. In front of the tree is Route 303, its guardrail shaded by apples.

What an incongruous site. In this industrial age, in this time of landfill pollution, water contamination and airborne disease, who would expect a tree to sprout in debris, grow with abandon and produce fruit?

How the apple tree got its start is a mystery. This section of the Thruway was built about 1953 and Route 303 was widened in the 1960s. However, the tree appears no older than 20 years.

I doubt if anyone notices the tree when it blossoms in the spring or when it gives fruit in summer. Drivers on Route 303 and the Thruway usually have only speed in mind. There is precious little time to stop and smell the flowers.

Trees, in children's stories, have spirit. They live allegorically, passing judgment, offering sage advice, befriending tots. If this apple tree, at the corner of the Thruway and Route 303 in West Nyack, N.Y. 10994, has such spirit, its mission in life must be to thrive in the midst of "progress." It stands in defiance of what we do to the land and the environment in order to forge ahead in pursuit of the good life and profit (at least for some).

The ultimate irony – and a lesson in itself – is that the tree is so situated, off two busy and dangerous roads, that you can't pick its fruit.
(October 8, 1985)

In a boy's Rockland

You can't say you're a country boy until you've cleaned at least one henhouse or walked through a horse barn. I've done both, and while I'm more a product of suburban-transition Rockland than its country days, I consider myself versed enough to be a hayseed.

My father, who also grew up in Rockland, can recall hayrides in high school (Spring Valley), but I never got to do that. We lived for a time in the Tallman area, long before there were any of the houses that now form the Village of Airmont, and behind us were the polo field and riding academy frequented by Burgess Meredith, Paulette Goddard and other Rockland stage and screen notables. There were plenty of hay and horses on the field, but I never got to ride a horse or hay wagon there.

On Saturdays, though, as a youngster in the second grade at the Airmont School (that old redstone building on Route 59), I would take off in full cowboy regalia – chromed six-gun, chaps, hat and all – and survey the fenced-in grazing fields. I'd find me a horse at the riding academy, pretend he was mine and give him bubble gum for his troubles. With the setting sun later in the day and the breadth of the open field, the scene wasn't unlike those in the Hollywood B-movie westerns then airing on early TV (1949).

The horse and I would eventually mosey on into the barn, where the hands would rub him down and I'd watch, all the while trying to keep the smell from overwhelming my senses. The stalls would be filled with horses and hay and the barn would be open at both ends to pull in and exhaust air. You couldn't help but feel close to these noble animals as they were bedding down for the everning while crickets offered a little night music.

The walk home, a short one for short feet, was delicious in its quiet – stars in the sky, horses rounded-up and Mom's good grub awaiting this tired pardner.

In other seasons I lived in South Spring Valley, which like the Tallman-Airmont area, is now a village of its own called Chestnut Ridge. In those days there were numerous henhouses along Old Nyack Turnpike, and no youngster went through life without playing in them, taking out the eggs and cleaning out the coops. Talk about smell. (If anything's routine, though, you get used to it; it's only in the recollection that things, like the sense of smell, are doubled.)

I had friends who either owned henhouses or knew someone who did, and we fellows, including Josef Bernard and Alan Gitlow, would trek down Old Nyack Turnpike to where the old South Madison Elementary School (renamed recently in honor of the late state Sen. Eugene Levy) now stands. There we'd hang out in the henhouses.

Hens are particular creatures, and you have to approach them just the right way or you'll get hen-pecked. You also can't abuse them mentally or physically or you'll upset the egg production. It's not child's play.

In even later seasons, my henhouse and horse barn haunts would be replaced by hut-building and playing in the many homes under construction in the county in the mid-1950s. The country that was Rockland was becoming less so with each new Cape Cod or split-level raised, and soon most of the horse barns and henhouses went the way of the old apple orchards.

They are just part of memory now, imbued in the experience of a life, the body of which is not yet complete. When that time comes – long off, I hope – I'll be happy to report that in its dawn there were trips to see a few fine mares and hens in a Rockland not so long ago.
(July 7, 1991)

A visit to a favorite library

It's a quiet Sunday afternoon, and you really don't want to go for a walk. Or maybe it's a weekday evening, and you've got to get out of the house. Where do you go?

Everyone has his/her favorite haunts, but in Rockland there are some special places that are on many people's lists – libraries. Each one has it own flavor; no two are alike. Each has it own director, with a style tailored to fit a particular view of what a local library should be. And each library has its own brand of patrons, whose likes and dislikes are reflected not only in the books in the stacks but even in the way the furniture is arranged, or how the bulletin board looks.

A library can be a most comfortable spot, even if you aren't an avid reader. It can be a home away from home, a place to hang your hat when you need to get away – from the family or the regular routine. You can find a favorite corner or chair or table and sit with a book or magazine or just your thoughts.

(This is not to say that libraries are just convenient resting spots when your soul needs it most; they are primarily suppliers of books and information. All of Rockland's libraries are good at this, and if I were on the town boards or otherwise in charge of funding, I'd give them a lot more money to work with.)

Libraries are much more than what they are, officially. In each and every one of these places there reside thousands of voices, some from centuries past, that can be heard in crystal clarity just by opening a page. By doing so, you can make many acquaintances, visit many lands, ponder the same themes that great men and common folk have for eons.

You can do all this from the comfort of an old wooden chair, in a well-lit corner next to a stack of books that smell as nice, in their own way, as did your grandmother's kitchen. There is the notion of comfort in these places. You're sure to feel right in your home away from home.

Rockland's libraries come in all sizes – from small, quaint hamlet ones to ultra-modern edifices complete with the latest in computers and book retrieval. While they are not all the same, while the patron of one might not be a willing visitor to another, all of the county's libraries are meccas of escape for many whose minds and hearts crave to be in touch with the voices – or the silence – within them.

(November 7, 1987)

Pop's store: Sweet memory

The ingredients are rather simple, and so are the tools. Yet I cannot make a cherry Coke the way "Pop" did at the Roth family store opposite the old North Main Street School in 1950s Spring Valley.

You would think that a few squirts of Coke syrup, a bit less of cherry, some seltzer and a twist of the spoon would do it, but it does not. There is one missing ingredient, and it must be in the touch, that bit of magic master chefs conjure up when they blend a little of this and that to produce a masterpiece.

Old Pop (I never did get his real name) didn't say much, just sort of grunted now and then as he shuffled back and forth behind the worn marble counter, glancing up when a youngster asked for a soda, an egg cream or, on very rare occasions since we kids did not have much money, an ice cream sundae. He seemed to have learned not to use his energy too quickly, because kids can waste your time until they make up their minds.

Most of the trade was for nickels and dimes – small sodas, large sodas or an ice cream Mello-Roll, the latter served mostly on Saturdays and Sundays when cleaning your room might get you an extra dime and a hefty appetite. Mello-Rolls were always anticipated with watering mouth, with eyes fully focused on Pop's fingers as he broke open the cardboard covering and popped the ice cream into a specially shaped cone.

As for the cherry Cokes, I used to get mine after a hot bicycle run from the old South Main Street School about a mile away. Even though I was living in Hillcrest, I still had friends in that section of town, where I also attended school, and went to see them from time to time. My way station, about halfway home, was Pop's. If it were winter, I'd use the occasional nickel in my pocket for three Bachman pretzels, always choosing the darkest ones because they were the crispiest. If it were warm, I'd get the cherry Coke.

Watching Pop make one, unlit cigar firmly cocked at 30 degrees to the right side of his mouth, was worth the nickel in itself. He'd take a small Coke glass, dip it in rinse water, squirt in the syrup and the cherry and then place the glass at a bizarre angle so the seltzer would hit its side rather than splash at the syrup. Finally, Pop would throw in a long-handled spoon, twist it around so you could hear it hit the glass and place the bubbling concoction on the drain board so it could settle down and more seltzer could be added.

He never seemed to measure anything. Not syrup. Not seltzer. Not mixing time. Yet the cherry Coke always tasted the same. And it always had a great aftertaste. The richness of the syrup lingered in my throat like fresh honey must have in earlier generations. My nickel went a long way.

Today, with Pop and his store long gone, I can't duplicate his mastery, nor can I find it elsewhere. Yet I can, on the hot days of the year, still feel the taste of a sweet memory. That's Pop's legacy to the kids of his time, and I am forever in his debt.

(July 7, 1994)

Nyack, gem on the Hudson

When Henry Hudson plied the river off these shores in 1609, he did not worry about a ferry, nor street parking, nor thespians, nor politics. But I bet he took in, albeit from off shore, the same beauty so many of us soak up in Nyack.

In nearly 35 years of varied newspaper activity, a bit more than half of them in Nyack's downtown at the paper's 1930-1982 home on 53 Hudson Ave., and with the rest so far spent intimately enough in the village as to call it a marriage, I cannot walk Nyack's streets nor look upon the Hudson without numerous frames of reference.

This is the town where longtime Journal-News reporter Virginia Parkhurst so thoroughly covered stories in balanced fashion that no one would challenge her on the facts. Sitting upstairs, almost tucked away anonymously in the meeting room of the old Village Hall on Main Street, she would take notes in longhand, then spend hours transcribing them into typewritten pages so she would have her facts straight before the story was eventually written. It was extra hours never balanced by monetary compensation.

The Nyack of my time, from the early 1960s on (but also the 1940s and '50s of my youth), was a newspaper town, with presses churning in the bowels at 53 Hudson so that the brick, one-story building, then two-story, then two-story with a large addition in the back, shook with the birthing pains of the daily effort.

It was the village where copy boys secured coffee for grumbling editors in the wee hours of the ayem, passing in quick pace the newspaper's first home on South Broadway or its second one on Burd Street (both buildings still stand). It was a community coming alive on the news of the previous night and day, and that day's too, with the menu already being written for the following day's meal, all to quench the appetite of Nyackers and other Rocklanders.

In the p.m., a toast could and would be made to the daily birth at the old Hi-Ho bar off Main.

Nyack was also the longtime home of the New York Telephone Co., with specially made, olive-colored utility trucks lining both sides of Main Street all the way up to the Lydecker Building. The switching frames in the edifice at Cedar and Main had wire pairs dating back to the late 1800s.

It was the village of a ferry to Tarrytown; a busy Main Street with some stores that had duplicates in Suffern, the other major shopping area in pre-mall Rockland.

This was Main Street, USA, with the requisite bakery, five and dime (two), sporting goods stores, dress shops, gin mills, diners and, yes, bookie joints and, once, speakeasies.

The Nyack of my time had all the flavor, sweet, bitter and in-between, of a typical downtown, and that served many tastes. It excelled overall.

But change came to Nyack, as to every community in Rockland and in the nation, and the village re-defined itself beginning in the mid-1960s as an antique mecca, a cosmopolitan suburbia with good restaurants, charming shops, renewal programs and all the politics, all the pull between old and new which that brings

It is a continuing stirpot of mixed feelings, and it sometimes boils over, this Nyack. As such, it is typical of Rockland and its never-ending change. That brings out more than enough anger and outright complaint.

But through it all, and as a result actually, Nyack has offered and does offer such a wide range of delicious flavor, with a great diversity of peoples, beliefs and sense of purpose and direction, that it is a truly wonderful place to live, to work, to visit. A gem on the Hudson.

I can no longer jump around the corner from 53 Hudson to Elliot's for a regular coffee at 15 cents per, and I don't much care for today's offering of mocha cappuccino espresso latte at $2 each, but the same goose bumps that often came to me early on a day when Nyack was again coming to life still rise on a walk down Depew toward the magnificence of Henry's Hudson.

And we still have newspaper people living there.

(August 18, 1998)

Sloatsburg: A community

Sloatsburg, a "small town," proudly uttered, has always been the No. 1 definition in this western Ramapo village's dictionary of life.

It may no longer be the rural land of Revolutionary War times or the early manufacturing community whose name was given to it by the Slot family, originally of Denmark; nor is it the town that in the heyday of New York Cityites traveling without a Thruway to the "Summer Alps" in the Catskills saw many a speeder caught by the late Police Chief "Teeter" Bill Conklin; nor is it the Sloatsburg of the 1960s and '70s, when the first crops of newcomers came to a village largely populated by the same families for many generations.

Yet, Sloatsburg has remained immune to the major suburbanizing change that has reshaped most of the rest of Rockland. Main Street, Route 17, has some of the same look of 50 years ago, and cars still whiz by too fast on the state highway. Miele's Restaurant stands as always on Seven Lakes Drive. The Ramapo River, Rockland's other major waterway, remains beautiful though compromised by a landfill and the Thruway, which took out a quaint gas station up from Miele's and put a big bridge over the road in its stead.

Even the realigning of the roads in the Palisades Interstate Park system in the late 1950s and early '60s did not impact the village much, bringing other traffic to Route 17, yes, but largely as the pass-throughs that Sloatsburg is used to.

When the out-of-towners are gone for the day, and the night comes to this land by the Ramapos and Torne Mountain, the same calm, the same woodsy feeling along the river, the same sound of crickets and scattering rabbits can be heard on the streets of Sloatsburg as they were by the five Indians who sold the land encompassing the village (then called Pothat) to Wynant Van Gelder in 1738.

It is an infectious feeling, this small-town atmosphere, and the fact that it has been adopted and strongly guarded by many a former NYC resident not used to the quiet night or scattering rabbits or crickets is proof indeed of the village's intoxicating nature.

Once a Sloatsburger, always one.

Wilfred B. Talman, the late and noted Rockland historian, tells us in "How Things Began in Rockland County and Places Nearby" that the last official thread of connection between Orange and Rockland counties after they separated in 1798 came at Sloat's Tavern. "At specified times, for a number of years, the supervisors of the two counties met at Sloat's to compare and reconcile their records of taxes, land transfers and mortgages." A memory to be noted in this, Rockland's bicentennial year.

And the bet is that when the Orange Countyites returned over the mountain from those sessions they did not feel all that different. For Sloatsburg has always been closer in outlook to that county than to Rockland. Get into Suffern and Haverstraw, and the change to a faster, more suburban, more fast-paced life begins to take hold.

It is no wonder that Sloatsburgers of today are itching too, as a proposal for major clustered housing travels the approval road. On another street, anti-housing residents are making noise, fighting to keep their small town image.

The curtain on the final act of that play is yet to fall, but if history is a guide, more Sloatsburgers than not will offer the message that while many pass-through motorists are tolerated on Route 17 and Johnsontown Road, those who would park their cars overnight in new housing would not be as welcome.

At least not if the small town has to become suburbia overnight.

(June 30, 1998)

148

Seeking the soul of High Tor

The early sunset of fall and near winter is best felt in the hollow of High Tor, near the transcontinental power lines and along the path that once led repairmen to the aircraft beacon atop the mighty trap rock mountain. It is both a chilling sunset, because the hollow is shaded, and a warming one, because the backside approach to High Tor is spotted with the brilliance of a still warm sun.

That time of year near the Tor is like the mountain itself – both warm and cold, inviting, yet distant to travelers. Mountains are much like people, and their souls are evident, if you care to take a look. The famous Indian in Maxwell Anderson's 1936 Broadway play, "High Tor," found the mountain to have such a soul:

"You must make my grave with my own people, higher, beneath the ledge (on the Tor)… And you must place me in the fashion used by the Indians, sitting at a game, not fallen, not asleep. And set beside me water and food. If this is strange to you, think only I'm an Indian with strange ways, but I shall need them."

The spirits rule on the Tor as surely as the Hudson flows beneath and beside Haverstraw. And the incarnated spirits of the present also exist. High Tor is a fairly well-visited spot these days, mostly because you can now get to both Low and High Tor by the hiking path from Central Highway. Before that road opened in the early 1960s, you either approached the mountain from the back, which meant a long, gradually steeper climb, or you tried for the face, which was never a good idea.

Either way, you had to contend with the snakes that seek the trap rock and their spots of warming sun and water that trickles from nowhere to somewhere. Joining them are a few deer, many rabbits and enough squirrels to make you go nuts. They won't really bother you when you hike as long as you respect their territory. Just as the mountain has its soul, these creatures, who have inhabited the Tor longer than man has, require dutiful regard.

In that, the mountain does not get its full due. Litter is found in the leaves, graffiti covers the trap rock and beer cans stand testimony to enough individuals who know nothing about woods, trees, ancient grass and the wind that whistles with a message through the rocks.

Sit on the Tor, early on an evening, and you will hear the wind. What it says to you will be found in how well you listen, but I'll tell you this: If you are even a bit sensitive, and if you let your mind fall open to what exists on the Tor, you will come away knowing that what God created is here for the duration.

High Tor is living, and it accumulates the effects of humankind – its good and its not so good. It stands witness to us all.

"There is nothing made," the Indian relates in the play, *"and will be nothing made by these new men …that will not make good ruins."*
(March 25, 1989)

One-lane tunnel and 'peace'

Anyone who has lived in Rockland after World War II has been aware of the "progress" dilemma. The county can't stay in place while the world around it grows economically, socially and culturally, yet what price are we willing to pay for advancement? And can we be sure that as we think we're taking two steps forward, we aren't really walking in place or going backward?

Some of us ask these questions every time an old home is torn down, or when farmland is cleared for development, or when we hear yet anew the 40-year drone of bulldozers as they plow through native clay and move Rockland's famous rocks to put up yet another video store, delicatessen or pizzeria.

Are we building too much? Are we building right? Are we taking seriously the Native American call that we must guard the land for our children's children? Or are we out for the fast buck, the convenient, close-at-hand store and the comfortable home no matter what the environmental cost? Are we in such a hurry that we level and pave over our heritage simply because it's easier than climbing the hills of good planning?

Now we must ask ourselves these questions once again. Over in Orangetown, on the famous Sickletown Road, there is a 19th century stone tunnel, one-lane, once meant for horses and wagons. It held up the mighty Erie Railroad, which helped open up trade routes to the Erie Canal and the Midwest through its Piermont-upstate New York run.

Some of the railroad is long gone now, first the victim of "progress" in Rockland, when cars replaced trains and trolleys, then subject to neglect and vandalism and finally, with its rails taken away for scrap, the right-of-way was left to wither to a narrow path when it long ago could have served as a wonderful, graded bike and walking route to Nanuet.

The next victim is slated to be the tunnel, which the county wants to tear down so that motorists do not have to wait in courtesy as a single car passes first. The idea is to spend $1.5 million (good grief!) on dismantling the tunnel and widening the section to make it two-way. Backers raise the usual rationalization: The project is 75 percent federally funded and 10 percent state, and the county taxpayers need not worry about the cost. So what? Aren't federal and state "aid" our money, too?

Orangetown is opposed to the plan. Its Town Board wants the county Highway Department to reconsider. Some residents say no, too, because they know the tunnel has charm, that it cuts down on speeding since it is a traffic control device and that any widening is sure to be too progressively modern. The county answers that there have been 21 non-fatal auto accidents at the tunnel in the past three years. Yes, and I'll bet they were all caused by impatient people. Will widening the road make them any less so, or will they just speed on to the next intersection?

A 1981 state Department of Transportation study found the tunnel had no established historical significance. What were the criteria? It was built more than 100 years ago, in the 1860s; it was crafted of local stone by artisans without benefit of power tools; it is one of only two working one-lane rail tunnels left in Rockland; and people have been honking or shouting their way through it for generations. That's historic enough for me.

Keep it. Spend $1.5 million on better things. Put signals at the tunnel, if necessary, to improve safety. It's good for motorists, including my impatient self, to slow down and wait as the quaint custom of "you first, then me" is observed. Progress? There's enough of it elsewhere in Rockland.
(July 7, 1992)

Roads not taken

One of the more useful things about growing up in Rockland and living here for almost 48 years is that I can crack a sinister smile and beat the newer-arrivals at the road game. Here they are, stuck on Route 59 on their way from Monsey to Nanuet, and they don't realize they could take Old Nyack Turnpike.

Or maybe they're fuming on Airmont Road, headed for Rockland Community College in Viola, when they could have used any number of less-congested side routes. Perhaps they take the Palisades Interstate Parkway straight to Bear Mountain, as all the city slickers do, when they could get off on Seven Lakes Drive, put it in neutral and coast four miles to the back parking lot near the ice skating rink.

Yes, being a native has its benefits. We may have to put up with all manner of change that we do not like, just like the people before us did when *we* brought change, but at least living in one area for a length of time earns you certain privileges. Like knowing the terrain.

That's not too difficult in Rockland anyway, since the county is small, its road system is not complex, and we have the dubious honor of having the Thruway and Palisades Interstate Parkway provide north-south and east-west local roads that make it relatively easy to get from here to there. Easy, that is, unless you go shopping on a Saturday or try to move during the lengthy morning and evening commuter rush.

I learned the local road system early on, through Sunday rides with my parents and grandparents. I furthered my knowledge through extensive driving when I got my license, and as a staff photographer for this newspaper for six years. I filled in all the holes, learning the quickest way to get from Stony Point to Orangeburg. These days, I take daily trips throughout Rockland for editorial and column ideas and to keep in touch with what's happening.

I'll also take to Route 59 early in the morning to recall what it was like to drive on an uncongested highway. I'll ride with the windows open on Pomona Road to remember summers there. Occasionally I'll even stick myself on the Palisades Interstate Parkway at the height of the rush hour to empathize with the harried masses.

And through it all and by virtue of my acquired road knowledge, I feel secure in the belief that if ever there's an Indian Point blowup, I'll know the roads to use – and they aren't the designated evacuation routes.

Pardon me my smugness in all this. I know it's small-town of me, but the one road I don't know is the one that goes out of town.

(March 13, 1990)

A hamlet's sweet fragrance

In the hamlet of Tallman, tucked away in the memories that the woods always harbor, is the distinct fragrance of apples ripe for picking. The early to mid-Septembers always brought a fresh harvest to old Cherry Lane, and young boys and girls, newly confined to school, had difficult time resisting the temptations of play in the orchards.

For both children and orchards, there are seasons, and the final season is long gone in Tallman – the few apple trees are but decoration on suburban lawns. No longer do the rows of ancient plantings angle off toward the Ramapo Mountains, maintaining centuries of quiet in the valley.

Cherry Lane, a main thoroughfare, remains, though – largely untouched by time and change. A busier road, yes, but one that when walked in the early morning in a half-mist still offers a view of the stream and lake, water that shortly fills the backyard ponds of the super rich in Saddle River. Here it passes through woods, where oaks older than the County Courthouse stand in majestic formation as the new unfolds.

Tallman, caught between Monsey and Airmont, is a quick passing, and the average Rocklander might not even know he/she has wandered through. Its claim to fame was long ago, in orchards and in polo playing, where the Hollywood and New York theater crowd spent Sundays in the country life of the '30s.

Now it is a hamlet of nice homes, good people and an elementary school far bigger than the several-room schoolhouse that once dominated. As a community, it, too, angles off toward the Ramapos, as did the orchards, and the sense is that it still is a valley of the quiet. Get off Route 59 and head down Cherry Lane, and you can lose yourself in a peaceful town.

In the Rockland of today, it is difficult to define the hamlets. Their boundaries are unknown to many, and the overlapping postal and school districts make people think you live where you do not. In Bergen County, you know that you reside in such and such a community because you have a downtown, a Main Street, a borough council. In Rockland, where the major growth occurred when the tract house was king, downtowns are strip shopping centers and the main streets are Route 59, and Routes 304, 306, 303, 202 and 9W, and the Thruway and the Palisades Interstate Parkway. Hamlets today are more or less confined to that which is betwixt and between the present and the past.

As such, Tallman is an enclave where the new exists – and well – and where the old still offers fragrances from a lovely past.
(September 13, 1988)

Monsey of the Munsees

If you are of a mind, you cannot walk Saddle River Road on a summer night without feeling the odd combination of spirits that are forever part of the Ramapo hamlet of Monsey. The Munsee Indians still seem to inhabit the sandstone caves in the Monsey Glen, the Erie Railroad's steam engines still seem to chug from Sparkill to Suffern, and the bungalow colonies still seem to thrive with summer dwellers.

This is Monsey; this was Monsey; this will be Monsey. Its heritage cannot be obliterated. Its flavor cannot be lost amid zoning squabbles and growth and commercialization and traffic. What made Monsey interesting for the Indians – the sandstone-lined glen near what is now Route 59 – remains uncluttered by modern man. Though overgrown, its terrain is unencroached, standing as a sentinel to a long-gone past that seems to come to life under the full moon of a warm evening.

Nor can Monsey ever lose the flavor of its bungalow days. In the late 1800s and peaking in the early 1950s, summer living in Monsey, with its fresh air, lakes, many trees and its nearness to Spring Valley's downtown, needed no advertisement. It was known; it was sought after.

Indeed, the many bungalows would help shape the village after World War II as housing needs were met by overlooking building codes and proper planning. This was not unique to Monsey, of course, and no blame is placed on anyone specifically. Monsey, like other suburban communities, was caught up in the urgency of modern living.

Originally, when the Erie came through in 1840, Monsey was to be called Kakiat, after the patent in that area stretching down to Viola. But a local judge reminded all that this was the land of the Munsees, and though they may be largely gone, their heritage must never be lost, and so the hamlet was named Monsey, with a modern spelling but the same sound. (This is why native Rocklanders know that you pronounce the name with a U, not an O, sound.)

Today, Monsey is a busy community traversed by two heavily traveled roads – Routes 59 and 306. Route 59 serves to divide the hamlet more than the other highway, with the community to the south picking up the flavor of

New Jersey as you head toward the state line. There is also more suburbia here, with parts of the hamlet more in tune with Airmont and Tallman and Chestnut Ridge. North of Route 59, to Viola, to Spring Valley, to Montebello, lies a Monsey with a particular religious heritage that dates back to the 1800s. It is a concentrated community that serves to exist in peace, to celebrate its heritage while being a good neighbor.

Modern Monsey is a mix of suburbia and tradition, of planning challenges and the right of peoples to exist in religious freedom. The Munsees are long since gone and their glen is no longer inhabited by day, but the spirit of communal gathering that marked their life thrives in the Monsey of 1990. (July 19, 1990)

Section Four
Various Themes

Winter coat, for one season

Once, now so long ago, when a winter wind chased fall away for just a night, a friend took from storage a camel-colored coat meant for the cold.

She threw it on and placed herself within, curling her shoulders inward and burying her hands in deep pockets, greeting not only the relief of instant warmth but also an old companion.

In those days, coats were meant for more than one season, and one did not have several. If you did not grow all that much, you greeted your friend like a long-lost buddy for an extra winter or two.

This was a nippy night, and the friend and I had shared some talk, which for us was like being near a running stream. At any given moment, either could dip into it and take fresh, new water, which never seemed to stop flowing, and exchange it with each other.

Always in a stream of consciousness, never at a loss for words.

Now, after years of occasional reflection, the subjects talked about so long ago are no longer of importance; they probably were not then, either, just part of friendship and an easy ability on each other's part to get along.

It was a time, that's all, and on this particular evening, winter had arrived in a tease, and the walk that I had set for myself back to my Hillcrest home awaited me with brisk breath. And no heavy coat of my own.

At 19, I was up to the walk, but my friend's father thought I should not hoof it, So he generously offered me a ride in an antique Cadillac that he took out on rare occasions, using the family auto for the routine runs.

With red leather upholstery and a super-quiet engine, and with me lost in the middle of a cavernous back seat, the several-street ride home seemed like a chauffeur-driven experience.

I could see my friend in the front seat, quite happy that she was with her dad, in this car, on a crisp night when youth and all promise awaited.

Before the car's heater could kick in, the camel-colored coat brought her warmth, a reminder of last season's comfort and the reassurance that it would continue, like her father's attention. She huddled in it like a down comforter on a snowy eve, content as the kitten who purrs when there is peace and quiet and safety and all things good in the moment, however fleeting.

The car drove on and the coat proved, for me at least, to be for one season alone.

(Oct. 29, 2002)

Rocker, another generation

This is the tale of a rocking chair, Mission style, circa 1922, that in 83 years has made its way from here to there, down to Florida for a while but mostly remaining in Rockland. It has been used for individual comfort and particular peace by a number of Gunther family members and others for all those decades.

It is a solid rocking chair, with old leather seat and large springs, rendered in the typical dark stain on oak that marked Mission style/Craftsman/Stickley pieces. It is not an authentic Gustav Stickley, the famed artisan who built beautifully designed furniture in the Arts & Crafts movement, but it has similar durability. Not a joint is loose in the chair.

When I was the smallest I can recall and it was summer, visiting or living in my grandparents' 14 Ternure Ave. home in Spring Valley, I would run to the enclosed porch and then jump up on the chair, rocking back and forth in the reassuring way a child does and to which, by human nature, we return in older age. As the years went by, straight into high school, the chair became my own spot in that home.

It was purchased, for a week's salary I bet, by my grandfather, Arthur Sr., for his wife, Maud, who was about to have my father, Arthur Jr., in 1922. He wanted her to have a comforting spot in which to rest and rock.

During World War II, Maud and probably Arthur Sr. at times, sat in the same chair on that wonderful porch, looking out at the Erie tracks across Ternure and worrying about a world at war and the loved ones in it. I am sure an assortment of cousins, an uncle and my grandparents' other relatives and friends took fine use of the chair and porch as well, each enjoying the wide seat, smooth rocking and other comforts of such a simple but reassuring and enduring piece of furniture.

My grandparents relocated to Florida in 1960, in part because even back then Rockland taxes had become too high for a man without a pension. Arthur Sr. had lost his job at the shuttered Briarcraft smoking pipe company in the Valley after decades there, and he and my grandmother moved South.

They and the rocking chair left my sight and went to St. Petersburg. I did not see the chair again until the later 1980s, after my grandmother passed on. It was the one thing my father wanted to bring back, understandable since he had been rocked in it before birth. It filled a nice corner in his Pearl River home.

There I would sit, decades past Ternure Avenue, a father myself, and talk to my parents when I visited in the 1990s. I would smooth away the wide arms of the chair just as I did when I was 5. As my mother's Alzheimer's advanced, I would sometimes clutch those arms as well, while conversation became more difficult in her enveloping fog. Patricia, my mom, died in 1999, and the chair then came to my home, with the strict warning from my father that I was not to restore it.

That I have honored, but the piece, so well kept by my grandmother and then my parents, and now my wife, Lillian, does not need restoration, again a tribute to the original design and maker.

Recently, our grandchild Isabella Frances Gunther visited our home in Blauvelt for the first time, and in a quiet moment when she was all mine, I tiptoed over to the chair from 1922 and sat down in 2005 to rock another generation of the family. In the chair where her great-grandfather was rocked. In the chair where her great-great-grandmother sat.

I wonder if the man who built this piece in a factory so long ago could have envisioned such a comforting history.

(September 20, 2005)

The bakery as living theater

The human condition is painted across a broad spectrum, and the slices of life so represented are revealed in the most unlikely of places. Take bakeries.

Cake and pastries are second only to my love life on the scale of what's important in this world. I'd drive miles for the right cream puff, a well-concocted custard crumb or a French apple pie. Having lived in the Rockland-Bergen region all my life, I have an entire route set up among the various bakeries that cater to the tastes of a particular day.

Others turn the TV set to another channel if the program doesn't suit them; or they take a walk or go shopping, call Uncle Louie in the Bronx or hit the video games for diversion. With me, it's often a quick trip to a bakery I haven't patronized for a while.

And that's where the slices of life come in. In Hackensack, N.J., for instance, there is a very, very old and wonderful German-style bakery just opposite Packard-Bambergers. This bakery has always had a fine trade, and Rocklanders learned of its goodies during the years when Hackensack and Paterson were major shopping centers serving Rockland-Bergen. This bakery specializes in custard crumb, exceptionally fresh and with the biggest, most solid crumbs you ever bit into. The shop is small, and in front of the counter there is a 6-by-2-foot section of worn-out floor, with six layers of carpet revealed, where customers literally have stood for generations.

The worn spot does not extend to any other section of the store – not to where the bread is, or the jelly donuts or the croissants. It's just in front of the crumb cake selection. After all, that's what the bakery is noted for and that's why people line up in front of the counter and wear the floor out.

In Ho-Ho-Kus, there is a small shop off Maple Avenue that makes cakes with real cream, but *one-half* the normal size. Why? Because many of its patrons are older people with no children. They want cake but not 22 layers. I once entered this bakery when it was super-crowded, yet a line had formed automatically, with no one fighting to get ahead of another. I saw an elderly lady behind me and asked her if she wanted to go first, but she replied, "Oh, No. We all should wait our turn." That was class. And you don't see it everywhere.

In Hillcrest there is an Italian-style bakery where I make an appearance every once in a while to buy its superb French bread. This bakery's offerings are as diverse as the area in which it is located. There are bagels, crullers and Italian pastries. It is multi-ethnic and reflects a metropolitan flavor.

Over in Montvale there is a bakery located among the small stores in a shopping center off Kinderkamack Road. Its owner is of European origin, Alsace German I think, and he offers lemon- and cherry-filled Danish pastry that must come from some Old World recipe. His customers are businessmen, housewives and school children, many of whom buy a cupcake here and a donut there. They eat on the run, to school, to the commuter bus, to the supermarket. This bakery is like a candy store, offering quick, tasty treats for patrons in a rush.

When I make the rounds at my bakery haunts, I try to observe the people a bit out of the corner of my eye. It's an interesting experience and never fails to offer variety – slices of life that sometimes delight as much as the pastries.
(November 26, 1983)

When we forgot the grunt

In some families, there is the forgotten child, or worse, the one who can never do right. I fear our nation did that to the Vietnam soldier.

These days, pride is clearly shown by most Americans for the ordinary serviceman or woman, even by those who do not support the war in Iraq.

The recognition is that these are brave, usually quite young men and women who willingly go in harm's way; who clearly express that they fight to protect each other but also the ideals of a nation; who, as the "embedded media" report, make quick friends with the Iraqis, recognizing that they are in an enemy land but that the people are not their enemy.

Any World War II soldier who was in the European or Pacific theaters could report the very same behavior and thinking. There wasn't as much stated reference to American ideals then, in an age where you kept your thoughts and emotions to yourself, but the beliefs were there.

This is "Saving Private Ryan" thinking, and it goes to the heart of relatively free American ways and caring. These are thoughts not always promoted by our government (witness economic and social neglect), but the goal is always in place. And most of the people do not fail as some of our leaders have and will.

In that, there is no better nation on Earth, though we owe an awful lot to some other countries for our beliefs and culture and surely the diversity that comes through our harbors to these shores and which continually rebuilds America.

So, where does Vietnam fit in all this? Why no parade way back when for the grunt who endured a hell as deep as in any U.S. war? Why was his uniform despised? Why was he called a "baby killer?" Why was he spat upon?

Why did it take a decade for the Vietnam vet to be recognized as a soldier, Marine, etc., who also put himself in harm's way, who also espoused American ideals?

Those who continue to debate the Vietnam War will tell you the ordinary military got caught up in the great distaste for a conflict that didn't seem to have reason or national support and which was never fought as a determined war anyway.

And Vietnam coincided with a time of national questioning. The youthful ideals of the Kennedy Age were turned sour by an assassin's or assassins' bullets in Dallas, and the once-comfortable feelings in Ike's middle-class America were no longer taken for granted. Unfortunately, Vietnam was part of the muddied picture. Unfortunately, men and women died there.

And men and women returning to our shores from Vietnam were branded as an extension of a government and a nation unsure of its roots and where it was going and how it was doing just about anything. Yet the soldier, Marine, etc., served as well as do those now in Iraq. What did he or she have to do with national direction? They were the cannon fodder of a country shooting but not looking.

These Vietnam veterans were unfairly treated, and as once the forgotten child or the one who could do no right, they were given emotional baggage that even a pat on the back and a bowed head years later cannot fully lift.

We Americans did wrong.

(April 15, 2003)

Coffee on a telling morning

A long time ago now, in another lifetime it seems, I used to drop by and give a friend a ride to school. Morning is always the telling time for people, and this person revealed much of herself at that hour.

Sleepy-eyed but carefully dressed, scrubbed and *almost* ready to do battle on yet another day, this A-student had just one requirement to meet before she opened the door, got in the car and went to the front lines: She had to have her coffee.

At 20 – I was 21 – she didn't seem "old enough" to be drinking coffee. I didn't yet drink it – milk was still my morning punch – and I wouldn't get into the delicious habit until I went to work for this newspaper and its grizzled news hounds a few years later.

At 21, I was used to making snap judgments. I was into opinions even then, and some – maybe most – were off the wall. Why should this friend bother with coffee, I asked myself. Is it a necessity of life? She doesn't smoke. She doesn't curse. She doesn't pick her teeth. Why should this pretty woman mess with such a strong brew? Obviously – I thought to myself – she didn't need it since she always seemed such a with-it, hardworking, level-headed person who paid her own way through college.

The answer would not come for years. Eventually, the ignorance that led me to equate drinking coffee with some adult function that is adopted only after age 40 caved in to experience and the education one gets from getting with it in the world.

You see, this young lady, at 20, was already with it. She was an honest person who was trying – and succeeding – at moving ahead in life. If her mother's good coffee – served in a large white cup, as I recall – helped put some fuel in the tank for another day, fine. After all, the car was loaded and ready to drive down the road of life.

Yes, morning can be a telling time. Some people are awake even if they're sleepy-eyed. Some are ready for bear once they get their morning coffee, or orange juice or whatever fuels them for takeoff. The point is that fuel is taken on when there is a flight to make, when you have a mission for the day, for life.

In my silly, little, silent criticism of a person's coffee drinking, I also offered a telling morning moment: Some are ready to go out and tackle the world; others haven't awakened yet.

But most of us grow in our own time and in our own ways. Eventually, just about all of us wake up and smell the coffee.

(December 11, 1990)

What's in newspaper blood

Every newspaper has characters straight out of the "Front Page," the famous 1928 play and movie by Nyack's Charles MacArthur and Ben Hecht. They are colorful sorts who do not fit any mold, who are creative geniuses even if they don't have industry pedigrees.

They are the ones who, like my predecessor Grant Jobson, are born copy editors: Give them a bunch of words and they can make the paragraphs sing, the lead entice and the ending punch. But don't try to sit down with them and ask for a dissertation on good writing. They know the craft by instinct and by absorption – from years of working side by side with other knowledgeable newspaper stiffs.

They are the ones like Barney Waters, an editor here in the early '60s, who bellowed across a room if he wanted you, mumbled under his breath about green reporters, hardly ever gave a compliment willingly but who lived and breathed the news business so completely that you drew yourself to his sweat in the hope something would make you look like a pro, too, rather than just wet behind the ears. And when he did grumble something like "Good, kid," you were on cloud nine, at least until his next bellowing.

Barney never fit a mold. He wasn't the type for corporate meetings or seminars. He wasn't about to argue with a page layout artist about the latest type styles or discuss media trends, all of which, it seems, are increasingly necessary jobs in the news business. As papers fight TV and busy schedules and lack of interest for reader time, surveys and reader interaction and consumer concerns become rightly important.

But I hope the Barney Waters and the Grant Jobsons and the Jimmy Breslins and the Tony Davenports and the unseen people in rewrite who have ghosted many a Pulitzer, and the beat reporter and the photog and the cantankerous editors still have their role. God made the Earth in six days and rested on the seventh. Newspapers give birth every day, trying to keep all of us informed and entertained. They make us happy, sad (and that can be good), angry, annoyed, inspired, and they make us feel guilty. They run the range of human emotions, each and every day, making us aware that we are, indeed, alive. To do that, they – newspapers – must also be alive. And it's the characters in the news business that have the most life.

Newspapers would be nothing but fish wrapper without the fellow and gal who show up at 2 a.m., tired from covering a long meeting or a child's illness or a tragedy and write from his gut and heart, ignoring the din of the newsroom, barely heeding deadlines and dodging the minefields that editors lay. The creative process knows no hours, recognizes no proper standards of behavior.

No matter how organized the news business becomes, its real success will always depend on the geniuses who can write, take pictures, pen the grabber headlines and zoom the pages to you with zest day after day, trend after trend.

Unconventional is the byword of real newspapering. May it forever thrive. (November 12, 1991)

A lifelong nurturer

It isn't easy to let go, but you really have no choice. Children grow up, and as they do, you step aside and let them bloom. They go off to colleges, careers and families of their own. Your part in their existence does not end, but it does change.

This growth is rational, ordinary and human, but the passing is not made any easier by knowing that. Take a son off to college, for example, and you're at once sad and happy, worried that he'll feel comfortable away from home and glad that he has an opportunity to do so.

You tell yourself that thousands of others have left for college and made it, that the majority have thrived in such an environment. After all, college is not just book learning, but a chance to meet other people, get along with them, exchange ideas, likes and dislikes. You think of all the kids that never had the chance, who had to work straight out of high school or, years ago, elementary school. You remember stories of 18-year-olds shipped to the Battle of the Bulge, some never to return. You tell yourself that people survive.

You also recall what you were like at 18. Your parents may have worried about you, but you never did. You were too young for such headaches, not old enough to pull down a closing shade of pessimism. The world was your oyster, and with health and exuberance, anything could be conquered. Things would always work out.

When you raise a youngster, the years go all too quickly. The child is kept safely at home, but even there you run to his/her crib to see if the baby is breathing OK. When nursery school begins, you tarry with the youngster until the teacher, with kindness and concern, tears you apart and you go off – alone for the first time. When kindergarten starts, you worry about school buses and your child's spending even longer days away from the home nest. Then comes elementary school and homework and you agonize over the youngster's abilities. Junior high brings concern about emotional and social development and high school means a driver's license and worrying about all the nuts on the road.

As a parent, you spend part of each day and night concerned about your child. That special interest does not end, ever, even when the child becomes 35, 45, 55. Like a farmer who watches his crops through the season, you are in the fields, watering, pulling weeds, fertilizing. You worry about whether there will be enough nourishing sun, whether a storm will threaten the crops.

The crops are thriving for most of us and, yes, they are hardier than we think. Still, we must tend them until the harvest.

And that is a lifelong watch.

(September 2, 1989)

Minestrone soup: Epiphany

I was having minestrone soup — Italian vegetable with pasta I'd guess you'd call it — when the epiphany came.

It was that slightly icy day we slid through recently, and I had trundled over the Central Nyack mountain at a snail's pace from West Nyack to Nyack. The trip took twice as long, and as soon as I hit Burd Street, I parked the jalopy and hoofed it to my destination: the HSBC bank. The tellers there always make my day since they are so friendly, and doing my business made me forget for the moment that the ice was everywhere.

I didn't want to make a run home to Blauvelt over the slippery slope of Clausland Mountain, so I opted for a bowl of soup at a Nyack pizza shop with great food but a decor that expired in 1975. (Who eats the walls, though?)

The minestrone was great — lots of vegetables, real hot (soup isn't soup unless it's very hot or very cold) and with al dente pasta, obviously homemade. And just the right prescription on an icy day. The fact that I could soak up a downtown and not a shopping strip for my walk to the soup repast made it taste that more delicious.

I'm not sure if the minestrone gave me the epiphany, but it could have, given its soothing quality, not unlike the first tomato Campbell's your mom had ready for you after that sledding in third grade. Whatever, I was mellow and the eyes were not as jaundiced toward people, places and things as this critic can be on a more acerbic day.

So, there I was, enjoying the couple-a-bucks soup as if it were $24 filet mignon with the 1924 chateau rouge, alone in the establishment when this older couple walks in. They're there for the soup too, it appears, because that was the kind of day it was, and the older you get, the more you go back to Mom's soup, even if you can no longer get it the original way. It's the natural course of events.

The couple sits down, and the waiter pops over to take the soup order. Only he really isn't the waiter. He's the fellow who throws the pizza dough in the air with precision, as if he has done it from birth. But the waiter (waitress?) hasn't yet arrived, this being the opening hour. So the pizza chef is the waiter of the moment.

As he takes the order, there is an interruption. His cell phone, tied to his apron strings (the phone is becoming an appendage for many), rings. Instinct volunteers his muscles to put the phone to his ear, even as he takes the couple's soup order.

It's humorous, for I've never seen a waiter take an order while also answering the phone.

I kind of think the couple must be annoyed, though, so I await their response. It's nothing. The pizza chef walks away, having taken both the order and answered the call.

Odd, I think. No complaint? Especially when complaints also seem to grow as we get older (maybe not enough soup for the soul).

Then I realize why there was no complaint. The senior lady takes out her *own* cell phone, perhaps inspired by the pizza chef/alias waiter, and makes a call, as if reminded to do so.

I slurp my soup in the worst affront to Miss Manners anywhere, anytime.

The epiphany: Life is like a . . . bowl of soup.
(Jan. 22, 2002)

Bags included arithmetic

Maybe it was inevitable that modern electronic cash registers would force grocery store counter clerks to give up manual arithmetic, computed on paper bags. But it is more than an art that is lost. It's a way of life now gone.

Once, our mothers sent us down to Mager's general store, or Roth's or Zimmer's, all in Spring Valley, or we went to Strunck's in nearby Westwood, N.J. Or, you went to whatever grocery there was in your village or neighborhood. We were dispatched to get milk, sliced cheese, butter, potato salad, etc.

The clerk, usually with white half apron tied about his waist, would hustle here and there in the store as other clerks waited on other customers. He would create a pile of your goods on the counter, separate from other people's goods. You could never figure out how he kept them apart from the piles for other customers.

"That it? '" he would ask, right arm already in the air, moving toward the small, sharp pencil he always kept behind his ear. He would whip that out quickly, almost in a circular flourish, pulling his arm straight as if in automatic adjustment, to begin tallying the tab. He might also twist his neck in reflex and place his left hand on the counter to lean his weight on it.

(I'm convinced this was the clerk's way of relaxing and taking a bit of neck-relief exercise until the next customer made him hustle anew.)

Pencil put to paper, it would hit a paper bag, also whipped out from the stack nearby. He would look at each one of your goods, recall the price, jot it down and then, also in definitive statement, draw a final line and add up the goods.

And, boy, could he add quickly. He would carry the columns in his head or write them on the paper, but in lightning fashion. No calculator needed. The tabulation finished, the clerk would yell out the cost, and as you gathered up the money, usually held tight and crumpled in your little fist, he would make yet another grocery clerk gesture by snapping the paper bag open so he could pack up the goods. It was the same bag used to add up your tab.

The bag snapped open each time without fail, always neatly. Then would come the roll of the bag's top, scrunched down so that bottles or paper cartons of sauerkraut, etc., would not spill. He would take your money, and then his hand hit the manual register so the price would come up on big tabs with a $ sign in front.

Change made, if there was any, he would lift the bag with one hand and hold the bottom with the other, advising you to take it from the bottom as well, so you could get it home safely and not have your mother mad at you.

This system worked whether the lights were on or not, since no electricity was needed for the calculator. It also made clerks good at arithmetic.

And for the customer? Well, it always seemed better to carry a paper bag than a plastic one, since you can't hold those without the goods moving about and turning upside down. And having the tab written on the side, especially if it was a long list of figures, was instant reaffirmation that you had some mouth-watering food ready to eat when you finally got home.

In today's hurried, material world, we can't always see how simple things add up in our lives.

(Feb. 23, 1999)

Not known, but understood

He was one of life's unannounced people, those who go unnoticed as they silently make their way through the years. You catch a glimpse of them from time to time, but it isn't until they are gone that you – in the still frames that memory flashes – recall such people.

By then the stills have brought you a mini-movie of the person and you are able, for the first time, to take notice of what was, after all, a fellow human being.

Frank was one of those people. He was a man of quite modest means, the son of Italian immigrants who never had much themselves. His education was bare and his job as a semi-skilled Western Union worker netted him little – sometimes too little for a family of two girls and a boy whose clothes closet never grew as fast as they did.

This man of 38 years, this balding, blue-collar worker approaching middle age and all that meant in terms of increased financial strain, teen-age youngsters and yet the warmth and reward of seeing his family grow, was increasingly happy in his small, old house. It was built in 1928 and cost him $22,000 when he bought it. It was one dream that came true for Frank. He probably thought of that when he was working his second, part-time job as a supermarket helper.

But while his workday may have been 12 hours, at least he wasn't in Jersey City anymore. There wasn't any tenement. His kids had a lawn to play on and good schools to go to.

Frank's children measured him well. The little time he had home with them never passed without a daughter or a son close by. It was the quality of his companionship rather than the quantity. When Daddy came home, he always received special attention.

One still frame catches Frank at the side of his house, his smallest girl – about 5 – chatting away nearby as he pulls weeds from the shrub area he knows full well he will never have time to cultivate properly. He isn't taking great joy in this, nor is he really bored. He hasn't time for that either. It's just that he's noticed the weeds and realizes he better pull them out before they get too big.

As Frank weeds, a neighbor's kitten gracefully pussyfoots by, lingers and rubs itself against the man's arm. A busy person might push the cat aside – because the wake is never wide enough for those in a hurry. A contemplative man might stop what he is doing and cuddle the kitten in his arms, giving it full attention.

But Frank just lets the cat nuzzle him, allowing him to go on after he has had enough.

That still frame was recorded by the eye and tucked away in memory's vault. It made little impression at the time, and didn't even register when two days before Christmas, with holiday decoration about, lights on up and down the street, the news came that the man's children would not see him this coming Christmas morning or any other. He had died after a heart attack while at job number one.

Some time later the still frame was flashed, a memory recalled. A flood of bits and pieces about a man hardly known fused together to give the deepest understanding possible of what one human being was all about. (September 17, 1981)

Where are the milkmen?

I don't think there will ever be as fine an alarm clock as the milkman. Not even roosters, whose dawn crowing is as subject to the mating call as is humankind's.

Neither rain, nor sleet nor snow stayed the merry milkman from his appointed rounds over the many long years of his devoted service, although today's preponderance of milk stores and greatly increased gasoline and labor costs have reduced the number of rounds the cow's best friend now makes.

There was a time when every street in Rockland had its own milkman, a true creature of habit who visited each house in distinctive fashion, knowing exactly where to leave the day's delivery, knowing precisely where he would find a note on the next day's order.

Long before dawn the milkman would be out at the distribution center, clinking bottles into the metal racks lining the walls of peculiar-looking trucks. With each route defined by time and experience, the individual driver knew when he would pass this house or that, round this corner or the next. Coming down a particular lane, his brakes would sound a familiar screech, and out of the open-door truck the milkman would bound into the half-darkness, half-light that is nature's eye-opener.

More often than not you heard the milkman hop onto your porch, the clink of his bottles echoing into the stillness. He was your alarm clock, your morning wakeup call.

The vanishing species that is the milkman was not only your deliveryman, but he took your orders – and he usually knew before you did what you'd want on any given day. Cream and two bottles homogenized for Mrs. Pfeffer on Tuesday. Mrs. Salvato takes chocolate milk Friday, the Rittbergs get cottage cheese Saturday.

Your milkman was also a confidante, a sounding board, a conveyer of gossip – sometimes a "yenta," sometimes not. If you saw him on his later rounds or if you were up early enough, he could fill you in on what was happening in the neighborhood. He didn't have to overhear a conversation or see an event – he merely noticed a car missing from a driveway, an early morning light shining upstairs to know there was something amiss. The milkman could also tell you how the night world was doing – how many accidents he had seen, who were in the diners.

Sometimes he would precede the other purveyors of foodstuffs – the Drake's truck, the Krug's driver; other times they would lead the deliveries on the street. They had their own world, these drivers, and one wondered whether they met nightly at some designated time and place to share – in a large picnic – each other's goods.

After the milkman dropped off his bottles into your milk box, his sleepy-eyed customers, in bathrobes and frayed slippers, leaned out the back door onto the porch to pick them up. If you were young, you beat your brother to the pasteurized milk that had the separated cream on top, drank the cream and left him the watery remains. The next day he beat you.

Sad to say, but on most streets the milkman has left our daily routine. Gone is our alarm clock. Gone is the sure start he gave us each day.

Gone, and not in a small way, and maybe that's why some of us are more grumpy than usual these mornings.

(July 31, 1982)

Stringing ideas on a line

Remember the laugh your mother gave you when, as a youngster, you took in the stiff-as-a-board wash from the backyard clothesline? The pants looked as if they had been in a press.

We do not see many clotheslines anymore, and my guess is that there are more busy psychiatrists and pharmacies these days partly because of that fact.

In a slower age (although my mother, who always worked as well as kept house, never had a "slow" day), everyone seemed to have a clothesline. In my youth, I lived in several sections of Rockland, including Sloatsburg, Tallman, Airmont, Pearl River and, mostly, Spring Valley and Hillcrest, and in each neighborhood there were many clotheslines or clothes poles, usually homemade contraptions built with whatever lumber was handy.

My mother's line was the ubiquitous white cotton twill, drawn through two pulleys and knotted. There was a line keeper, which helped prevent sag, and, of course, the usual canvas bag full of clothespins, preferably spring-loaded. Trees served as poles.

Every Saturday morning in the 1950s, on what was everyone's main wash day in Hillcrest, this lazy fellow would be awakened by the squeak-squeak of the pulleys as my mother hung the wash. It is a sound that, to this day, recalls the peaceful weekend lounging of a teen-ager. I just rolled over and went back to sleep.

My mother would take her time hanging the wash. It almost seemed like therapy of a sort for her, time to get out of the house, to feel the fresh breeze, to smell a new morning and to let her thoughts just move about her head. In that, as she sorted the wash, she also seemed to sort out her thoughts, and I do not doubt that it gave her a sanity boost.

At other homes, where the clotheslines might be closer together, there was over-the-line talk between neighbors, and for many this became a ritual not to be missed. Gossip was exchanged, hopes were defined, news was spread. If a photographer could have spent some time at such a clothesline gathering, he could have captured facial expressions ranging from interest to skepticism to wonder to joy to sadness. But almost never boredom.

I'm told that in the old New York City neighborhoods, where buildings' rears met in a courtyard, there would be a central pole to which were attached many pulleys carrying lines from second-story unit windows. What gathering spots they must have been, with enough news daily to fill a weekly paper.

And, of course, everyone would know everyone else's fashion. When you hang it all out, including your underwear, that's not hard to miss.

My mother used to carry the wash in a straw basket, which she had for many years until it literally fell apart. When I first carried it out for her, as a little fellow, it was so heavy that I could hardly do so. By the time I was a senior in high school, it was so light, and my knowledge so sure that I would not be doing that chore for many more years, that I wished for a moment that it was heavy again.

You do not see many clotheslines anymore, with dryers in homes and with people too busy to take time for such labor. Life seems too quick for passing, even absent, thoughts, strung along a line ready to evaporate, as with the water in the clothes.

(July 15, 1997).

The 'Greatest Generation'

One of the odd things about life is that people who seem ordinary are sometimes gems hidden from us.

They go about their lives as we do, and in the usual circumstances, they have ups and downs and achieve here and there, but otherwise seem just like the rest of us: dependable, all tying our shoes in the same fashion.

But not really exceptional.

Back in the 1960s, I worked with a fellow named Ken Harniman, an agreeable, helpful sort who passed on some good newspapering to a neophyte. In time, our reporter, business editor and copy editor left the paper for other jobs, some in other fields. From all reports, Ken was the same solid, dependable colleague he was here at The Journal News.

In the 1960s, we knew that Ken was involved in many veterans' groups and doings. But so were some of the other men and women at the paper, this being less than 20 years since the end of World War II. We also knew that Ken had been in the Army Air Corps; however, most at The Journal News had been in some branch of the services.

So, nothing extraordinary.

I would not learn until some years later that Kenneth F. Harniman, once of Nyack and for many years a Nanuet resident, had been shot down over Europe, sent to a German stalag luft camp and escaped. That he wrote many vignettes, some 500, about his experiences, any of which could be movie plots in themselves; and that he had more than a lifetime of experience by the time he was 29.

He was a captain in the Air Corps, later the Army Air Force and then the separate Air Force. Ken was lead navigator, 8th and 9th Air Force, 322nd Bomb Group, 451st Bomb Squadron, flying B-26 "Marauders."

On his 52nd mission, two before he was to rotate home, Ken and his crew were shot down over France while bombing a V-2 rocket site. He was captured by the Germans and spent a year in Stalag Luft III, near Nuremberg.

Once at camp, he wrote a one-page newspaper to keep fellow prisoners savvy on the war's progress, with facts gleaned from new prisoners. He and others also sent air targets back to the Allies via an underground network.

Ken escaped near the very end of the fighting when he and his fellow prisoners were taken from the camp, then being approached by the Allies, and force-marched toward another stalag for about 100 miles in terrible weather.

He found refuge with a family of sympathetic German farmers but was later recaptured.

Before he had all this living crammed into him during World War II, Ken was a Nyack High School standout in the early 1930s in track and field, cross-country, football, basketball, tennis and bowling. He was recently inducted into the Rockland County Sports Hall of Fame.

After the war, besides working at The Journal News and in other places, Ken handled public relations for the Rockland Veterans of Foreign Wars and engaged in all manner of community activity.

But, you know, when he was at The Journal News, he was just unassuming Ken: affable, modest, humble.

Yet fate gave him a heavy role in the war, and the hat's off to him for assuming it so responsibly and bravely as a member of the "Greatest Generation."

(May 21, 2002).

1944: A fellow doing his job

There are anniversaries for all sorts of reasons in most people's lives, and some are observed more than others. Sometimes it's not even the individual involved who does the observing.

Such is the case with my uncle, Winfield A. Gunther, who once, long ago, lived at 14 Ternure Ave. in Spring Valley, and who, 50 years ago this month, was seriously wounded in the Huertgen Forest campaign just prior to the now famous last German offensive of World War II, the Battle of the Bulge in the Ardennes region of Belgium, France and Luxembourg (Dec. 16, 1944 through Jan. 31, 1945).

Fifty years ago is a long time back, too, but I do not know if the five decades are just yesterday for my uncle. He does not talk of losing fingers on his right hand after being pinned down under rapid fire with other U.S. soldiers. All he has said is that he would never forget the day he was wounded, for it was his son Jimmy's birthday.

Winfield Gunther is not unlike most ex-soldiers you meet. They don't talk of war, of killing and the fear of being killed. While the bragging rights are theirs for surviving, for serving their nation in a just cause, I can only guess (since I've been spared the experience) that all men in war, friend and foe, are fellow human beings who have jointly walked in hell. There is no cockiness for the ones who happen to come back.

My uncle is also a typical American, both of his generation and for all time. On the latter point, we are a forgiving people, and that's why our memories for hate are short. We are friends now with former enemies, and we were that soon after the war.

As a typical American of his generation, Winfield Gunther lived through the Great Depression, saw his father (my grandfather, the first Arthur H. Gunther) work long hours at low pay to keep his job, went off to join the Merchant Marine though he was underage (in part to lessen the family burden) and eventually married and had children before he was drafted in 1944. It was then that the nation was readying for the advance to the Rhine and the end of the war in the European Theatre.

The government, in all its wisdom, put this former experienced sailor in the Army, the infantry no less, but my uncle blended in with the other grunts and set about to do the job and get back home to civilian life. He was the typical American civilian soldier, the fellow who left the farm and fought in the War of Independence, or who went to Gettysburg or to St. Mihiel, the Huertgen Forest, Inchon and the deltas of Vietnam.

These are the men (and women) the late Ernie Pyle, the truest, most accurate of all soldier/sailor/Marine commentators, celebrated in his still-moving columns filed from the front. Read his work and you will see, hear, feel Main Street, USA, Mom, Dad, people of all ethnic and religious and racial backgrounds. You will know their fears, shed their tears, understand their humanity and decency.

Winfield Gunther was in that sea of good people that Pyle wrote about. Unannounced by name, almost anonymous on purpose, he went where he was told and did what he was supposed to do. He never expected anyone to say thanks because he was just one of many called to the task then at hand.

But after 50 years, I note an anniversary and say thanks.

(December 13, 1994)

When nature steps in to help

In the early morning, on a day when you're not hell bent for rushing about, in the hours when your pulse is normal and your step, while lively, is not doubled or frenetic, it's possible to hear more than the birds sing. It's the beginning of a day in the slow lane, one in which you let the others whiz by.

These days don't come too often for most of us. There's always something to do, some task to be performed, and it has to be done an hour before you'll eventually get to it. Rush, rush, rush – that's the sort of existence many of us endure. And it's not just the workers among us who become harried – sometimes frustration alone, frustration over anything, can do it. You can be retired and on the edge at the same time, or a young person who has much ahead of him, but at the moment, there's just too much to do and all seems hopeless.

It's during these times when, every so often, nature steps in, deliberately, carefully turning down the high-pressure valve, dropping the idle to below-normal rpms, shifting you into neutral just when you thought you were ready once again to step on the gas at yet another green light.

No new intersections today, though. The fresh morning, with the smell of summer's humidity and a dew that glistens as a bright sun hits the dark green grass, offers a quiet start and the promise of more to come this day. Sure, you may have to go to work, or run errands, or get upset by this or that, but since the gas under the kettle has been lowered, nothing's going to boil.

We run into this calm infrequently, not enough to suit our tastes or meet our needs, but enough to make us confident it will come again. That's a treat to look forward to, just like the ice cream soda you knew you were going to get as a kid after you went to the movies with your parents.

It's such a rare feeling, in fact, that many of us can recall when we've had the moments. It may have been on a walk somewhere, say on South Mountain Road on a summer night when there are no cars in sight and the darkness offers an umbrella over your cares while the steady, bubbling sound of the mountain brooks ensures a calming rhythm. Or maybe it's a moment with someone you hardly know, but who makes you feel immediately comfortable. Or perhaps it's a few hours with a young child, when you realize you are with someone who has not yet lost his innocence and who has yet to become part of a busy, dangerous world.

Or maybe the quiet time comes just as you are about to fall asleep, and you, in the safety of your bed, know you have made it through yet another day and survived. Now these minutes are yours alone, to dream as you can when the sun is down and you're free to travel anywhere with your thoughts.

Or, for me, maybe it's a moment like this, when I began to write a column on another subject, one that I've already forgotten, but instead my mind has turned to these descriptions. Nature has put me in the mood, and I think I'll enjoy the moment.

(June 6, 1989)

Everyone needs a *schmatte*

Maybe you received a beautiful sweater for Christmas. Or a tie. Or a blouse. Where did it go? In the drawer, to be saved for a special day or evening?

If you're like me, you filed it somewhere. Not that you or I don't like to wear new things, but for some reason when other people buy them, we smile, receive and appreciate them but then somehow distance ourselves from the present for at least a decent period. Maybe we feel guilty about getting a present. Maybe we don't think we deserve it. Maybe we like to hoard things for a rainy day. Maybe we don't need a new tie.

Or maybe you're really in my league. I'm not the bum of the year, but I have become attached to certain sweaters, an old hat or two, even quite used socks. Perhaps I associate them with good times or good luck or someone's good will, but time after time I will bypass the $50 maroon sweater in favor of a threadbare, off-red *schmatte* that I've had for years and which cost maybe $8 when new.

Schmatte. (Also shmatte, shmate.) That's a wonderfully descriptive Yiddish word, one of the many I learned while growing up in the Spring Valley of the '50s and its summer bungalow world. It describes, especially when you say it with traditional zest, any old garment that you wear when the neighbors aren't watching. It's what you put on when you want to let your hair down but still be legally clothed.

I also have an old Mets baseball cap that once belonged to my younger son, way back when he was six. I'm not a Mets fan, but I wear it because I've stretched it to the point where it is quite comfortable. I may look silly in it, but I don't march in parades with the hat on, and what I do in the privacy of my home is my business, right?

Certain old socks hold a lure for me, too, and shoes as well. Perhaps the oldest garment is a tie that I wore to my high school graduation and on my first visits to the Bear Mountain Inn. It is so thin in width that it may be years before it's back in style, but I'll keep it anyway.

Maybe there should be a special place where we could bring our schmattes for renewal and rejuvenation. The threads would be resewn, the colors brightened, the look restored. That way we could run out in full view of everyone, wearing our best, *old* clothes.

But don't box them in fresh, new packages. Don't make them look so new that they are no longer our friends. After all, when you come home in a blue funk, or you're tired and don't especially want to see or talk to anyone, you want some inanimate acquaintances about, like an old sweater that you can get cozy in and won't talk back.

Everyone needs a schmatte.

(January 27, 1990)

Fight on for the fallen

A date that has already lived in infamy for a year is recognized today on its first anniversary.

It is not like any other day that is simply recalled on its annual date. Has anyone in this nation, in this Rockland, despite attempts to the contrary, stopped thinking about Sept. 11, 2001, and the terrible, unprecedented physical attacks on humanity; on the World Trade Center, the Pentagon and airliners; on these United States?

Have we come to closure over the mental anguish and the disbelief that this nation and its people were so savagely attacked?

No country deserved this horror, though other nations, in other times, have suffered horribly as well, losing thousands in a single day. And our United States has seen thousands pass before, too, in one setting, at Pearl Harbor, at Gettysburg, in the devastating, mind-numbing battles of World War I, in the Huertgen Forest in late 1944, in the Pacific campaign.

But all that was about obvious war and a demonstrated enemy, even if the enemy was ourselves at Gettsyburg.

This time, in the new war of sometimes faceless terrorism, all citizens are soldiers and are forever on alert, perhaps forever at battle.

That is why we cannot forget, why even today, we are observing yet another 24 hours in memory since Sept. 11, 2001.

We add to that memory daily as more names of the fallen, of those who died in great honor for us — our police, firefighters, the not-so-ordinary citizenry — come to mind.

This is a human story that will long be told, as if the souls who perished will not easily rest until it is repeated over and over.

We do not yet know what the story will fully read, for parts are not written.

Will there be war with Iraq?

Will there be deepened international conflict? Will our economy suffer? Will our young die again?

Will our way of life continue to change through added security measures?

Will we guard our constitutional liberties even as we see the necessity of a tighter ship?

Largely, then, it is we, the survivors, who will, who must, write the story post-Sept. 11, so that those who died will rest in peace, so that they will not have died in vain.

It is the great hope of humankind that we do the right thing, for this time the physical safety of all life rests in the nuclear balance. War begets war, and death brings more of the same in repeatedly used killing fields.

When the smoke clears and the fields are washed of the blood of the latest to fall, another conflict always seems likely. But not inevitable. This will be the story and the challenge of humanity until this Earth's end. Horror, or the potential of it, must always be addressed, for to neglect that duty is to invite holocaust and destruction.

Yet, as Gen. Douglas MacArthur well knew, you choose your battles, to save lives, to effect the best outcome.

And you forever stand guard, firing the weapon or not, with the spirit of many souls upon your shoulders.

Fighting on as the living, we must do fully well by those who have passed on.

So it is with Sept. 11 and today's memorial and the memorial of every day after Sept. 11, 2001.

Recall Abraham Lincoln at Gettysburg: "But in a larger sense we cannot dedicate — we cannot consecrate — we cannot hallow this ground. The brave men, living and dead, who struggled, here, have consecrated it far above our poor power to add or detract. . . .

"It is rather for us to be here dedicated to the great task remaining before us . . . that we here highly resolve that these dead shall not have died in vain; that this nation shall have a new birth of freedom; and that this government of the people, by the people, for the people, shall not perish from the earth."

Let us do the right thing. Otherwise, the terrorists will have won.

Post-Sept. 11th must be the consecration of the fallen.

(Sept. 11, 2002)

Wind-up clocks kept us sane

Why is it that with more time on our hands we have a quicker pace of life?

Consider your grandparents, or maybe even your great-grandparents. Your ancestor went to bed early, maybe 9 p.m., perhaps after listening to Jack Benny's radio program. But first he had to bank the coal furnace to keep the house at 55 degrees through the night and make the morning fire start easier. He got up early because of that and maybe because he had to care for the few chickens he might have, or perhaps he had to pump water from a well and stock the wood cook stove for breakfast. He shaved with cold water and a razor.

Your grandfather or great-grandfather made many motions in his daily struggle – shoveling coal, winding his alarm clock, then his watch, getting the milk from the front porch, maybe even turning over the car motor by hand. Perhaps he walked to work, where there were no computers to make things easier. He did lots of repetitive tasks on the job too.

After a long day in what was sometimes a six-day work week, he came home to grandmother, who perhaps made her breads by hand, cakes certainly. No microwaves. No pre-packaged foods. Also, no one on the run, eating at his or her own pace. A family dinner, with all the members gathered, was the norm.

Grandmother did her hair with a curling iron heated by the stove. Maybe she didn't have an electric iron, either, but a cast iron one that also needed to be heated. The wash was done by hand and wrung out through a roller and then hung on the outside clothesline, even in winter when the cold would make the clothes as stiff as a board.

Grandmother would jar fruits and vegetables in the late summer and fall, harvested from grandfather's garden, an added task for him in the spring and summer. The lawn was cut with a push mower and the dandelions sliced out by the roots with a pocketknife.

Both grandparents might take a walk on a summer's evening, when the day was long, and look in the windows downtown. Or there might be another radio program, with a newspaper to be devoured cover-to-cover by grandfather while grandmother sewed. Weekends – Sundays at least – neighbors dropped by to say hello or to play cards.

All in all, a relatively quiet, well-oiled, smooth existence with many tasks to do each day. Was it better than today, with our electronic gadgets, quick food preparers and other time-savers? Certainly life now is not as hard physically, and it is more comfortable. Your grandparents and great-grandparents would have welcomed modern heating and kitchens.

Yet I wonder if living today isn't more of a trial mentally. Our time-savers have given us more time, but what do we do with it? Find more places to run off to, more things to do, more subjects to worry about. The calm reassurance of repetitive tasks is not as common now, and sometimes not having a clock to wind gets us all wound up inside.

(June 30, 1990)

Blessing came twice

People have a right to brag about their children, though it should always be in such understatement that it is in good taste. None of us want to see endless pictures of the kids, or if you have them, the grandkids.

Yet there are moments when there should be applause, not because the person deserving it is your offspring, but because a human accomplishment has been made, and it should be recognized.

Herewith I acknowledge Andrew Edward, my second son. Like the first fellow, Arthur 4th, he is an athlete, particularly a runner of long distances.

But Andrew is also a swimmer and a bicyclist, and like his mentor, Coach Bob Hudson of the South Orangetown schools, he recently chose to enter the "Tin Man" race in upstate Tupper Lake. That event is cousin to the famous "Iron Man," in which participants swim, then bike, then run a long distance.

In the Tupper Lake Tin Man Triathlon, held in late June, participants had to swim 1.2 miles, bike 56 miles and run 13.1 miles, all in succession. Andrew came in 116th out of a field of 705, with a time of 4:56:42.

Now, I am a walker, but my limited 4.5-5 mph daily jaunts are just a whisper in such a strong voice of almost five hours of unending endurance.

To say his parents are proud is an understatement; to say he is my son is even more a thanking of the gods.

When you are a parent, you hope your children will be more successful than you, as students, as siblings, as careerists, as good human beings. You also hope that they carve out individuality, that they be something special for themselves and for existence.

I must now report that, all my mistakes to the contrary, these two fellows, Andrew and Arthur 4th, have bested expectations a hundredfold. In that, I also applaud all parents who have been given such gifts.

I once thought that my oddly eccentric ways and early-on mistakes would preclude me from the company of such offspring. Somehow I lucked out, and I'll give that blessing to God and the boys' mom, Lillian.

I'm just happy the fellows have been in my life. While a triathlon or a marathon does not a person make, there has been equal success in other, more vital areas of the lives of these two men.

I know the endurance, dedication and purpose of the long-distance runners are also the mantra of their jobs and lives.

I owe the big guy up in the sky a great debt for these two.
(July 16, 2002)

Recalling a mom's quiet ways

How do you sum up your mother's life when she passes on, as my mom did last week? How do you pay tribute to someone who helped form the better parts of your character and who, even in death, gently reminds you of your failings?

Each of our mothers is different, and we each interact according to our own needs and the personal emotional ties formed. I was particularly close to mine, this quiet, shy, hard-working woman born of an Irish mother and an English father.

She rarely scolded, knowing that her equally shy son had to find his own way, and that while he stumbled often enough, he could surprise her with a reservoir of strength and renewal that could only be initially filled and inspired by a mom who deeply loved and cared for her family.

My mother was born in 1918, fittingly on St. Patrick's Day. She and her two brothers, John and William, were the only survivors of the 13 children of John and Mary Lyons. Childbirth complications and the worldwide flu pandemic of that time took their lives, and their deaths made even more somber a household already beset with difficulties.

When Patricia Joan Lyons was just 6 or so, she woke up one morning next to her 32-year-old mother and saw that this woman, too, had left this earth. Then it was off to an orphanage for a year and finally to an aunt in Queens, where she stayed until 16. A child of the Great Depression, she had to find work to support herself and family, and, except for the time spent having my brother Craig and me, my mother worked until her retirement in 1983 from Lederle Laboratories in Pearl River.

She worked all those years, even with my father holding two, sometimes three, jobs so that we could have our homes in suburban Rockland and so her children could have professional careers. She never complained about her workload, which I, for one, did not appreciate enough. As a teen-ager particularly, I did not recognize the sacrifices she and my father made.

But we do not usually see our parents' worth until they get old or pass on.

When I was in the sixth grade, and we were living on Karnell Street in Hillcrest, my parents had gone shopping on a particular Saturday. My room, shared with my brother, was then on the first floor, and I was alone in the house. I walked into my room, flopped down on the bed and began thinking about this or that, as a 12-year-old will do.

In a flash, and with my skin tingling, I realized I was growing up and that some day my mother would be old and would pass away. I cried in that moment for the first time for my mother's mortality, and now I cry again at her passing.

Yet, I am grateful for this earthly leave-taking, for my mother suffered from Alzheimer's disease for at least the last eight years. My father valiantly took care of all her needs and suffered the indignity of it all until late in 1995, when we convinced him that, for the sake of both parents' health, my mother would best be cared for in the new Alzheimer's unit at the Dr. Robert L. Yeager Health Center in New Hempstead.

This wonderful county facility took great care of my mom, and we would make it a habit to go up there, my father, brother and I. It was a family bond renewed from the days of our living together in Spring Valley, Hillcrest, Sloatsburg, Nanuet, Tallman and Pearl River, and we hoped our mother somehow knew – from a touch, from a look – that we were together again.

Patricia Gunther's last months were not the best. Alzheimer's is an insidious disease, and it first ate away her thinking circuits in the brain and then those that control bodily functions. It is a slow death, one that can strike anyone, and unlike the parent who dies from a heart attack, there is no sudden departure.

You watch the person slip away, and the time is so lengthy and the mental and physical changes so severe that you begin to forget what the relative looked like, how she spoke, how she interacted.

It is only now, in looking back at old photographs, and in the private moments of reflection that the death of a loved one brings, that I see my mother again as the caring mom she was. She never complained about her early hardships, never even missed a day of work in any job. She wanted her family to succeed. And she did all this as a quiet, simple person.

She did not even talk much about her own mother and the childhood she did not have. In an age where so many people make excuses because they are "deprived" or have this or that liability, my mother stands out for being so selfless and for getting on with life for her family.

My heart hurts. My mind is numb. I am at a loss without my mother.

But I am immensely happy that this salt-of-the-earth woman has gone to her reward. Now in that great land called Heaven she can hug her own mother at long last.

(January 19, 1999)

A fraternity of life and death

How small so many of us seemed at a recent showing of the moving World War II film "Saving Private Ryan." How small you can feel when you are not of the "fraternity?"

We went to see it the other day, almost as a pilgrimage in the current re-interest about a war more than a half century ago. Steven Spielberg's movie has been hawked as a more accurate look at "the last good war," showing it for the hell all war must be. Like the recent HBO film about the disastrous Hurtgen Forest (1944) campaign on the Belgian-German border that resulted in some 25,000 American casualties, "Saving Private Ryan" is a GI's view of war.

For years, Hollywood "protected" us from truly bloody scenes. Military personnel died, but we did not see them blown up, with limbs scattered and intestines floating in water at landing beaches.

We did not hear the never-ending clack-clack of machine gun fire, nor the mortars nor the whiz of cross fire.

We did not smell death or the cheesy odor of gangrene-set limbs. We were not engulfed by the urine-soaked stench of men so frightened they lost it in their pants.

But in the Huertgen Forest movie and in "Saving Private Ryan," you see, smell, almost feel the horror of battle.

Almost feel, that is. Here we were in a suburban movie theater, in a building that could have risen only because America won the war.

Yet the last time some Rocklanders saw the West Nyack swamp, on which the theater now stands, in which a movie about them was being run 50-plus years later, was when they were on their way to the Nyack Selective Service Board, then to the European or Pacific theaters. Maybe to D-day and the landings at the Utah and Omaha beaches. Maybe to death on the Normandy shore.

Watching "Saving Private Ryan" was a riveting experience, not because I savor anything about war. I was there simply out of curiosity and because, as a historian and as a human being, I want to understand what other times were like.

But I realized that no matter how close Spielberg came to honesty in his magnificent portrayal of the brutal hell of it all, as well as the comraderie of men of various backgrounds and beliefs thrown into such a situation, I could never be part of it.

I was not there on the beaches on D-day, nor was I even in any Army or Navy or military situation. It is a fraternity closed to me, most especially the fraternity of battle death. Ironically, for that, I and others must thank those who died in such terror.

The film's run was nearly three hours, and you could hear a pin drop in those many moments when the sounds of war, sounds of what it must have been like more than 50 years ago, were greatly amplified in three-dimensional effect.

This was not a popcorn film either, for how can you munch when a man's arm is blown off and he stops in bewilderment to pick it up?

The audience contained many people of the World War II generation, men and women, and my mind kept going to what their thoughts might be. Were women understanding for the first time the hell their husbands never talked about?

Had they lost young husbands or brothers on those beaches?

Were any of the men there on D-day or after?

Just as the movie was about to go to its credits but before the house lights came up, I saw three men who seemed to be in their 70s slowly make their way to the exit as if they had to leave in anonymity, almost like the comrades of war. Their eyes appeared misty, as were the eyes of many of us in that audience.

One fellow paused at the exit, hidden from the view of most, and just stared at the closing scene. He looked lost in thought, perhaps transported back to a moment in time shared with those men portrayed on the screen.

He seemed part of the fraternity.

God bless him. God bless those like him in any war.

(August 4, 1998)

Life defined on a snowy night

I believe there are glimpses into Heaven in this earthly existence. Once, for me, it came on a snowy night during a walk to Monsey and Viola in a snowstorm.

It was February 1962, and life was good enough at age 19, halfway to 20. I was healthy, young, full of vigor and hope and dreams, though I was surely confused about almost everything.

What would become the lowly beginnings of a long career at The Journal News was two years away, and I was about to take courses at Hunter College in the Bronx, though my mind was not on that sort of learning. My friends were away at school, and a great quiet had entered my life at this point, since I had a lot of time to myself.

I wasn't particularly looking forward to school in the city, for I was, and am, a semi-country boy. If I had my druthers, I would have begun some sort of career right then and there, so eager was I to do something, though I had not yet been steered into that something.

So, on this night in February 1962, in the great quiet of my young life when I seemed to be sensitive to every sight, sound, word and view that I now realize would become the font of all my work at this newspaper (a "college" education in itself), I sat at home in the attic rooms of my parents' house in Hillcrest.

It was about 7:30 p.m., and I glanced out the window. On what had originally been a mild day, with temperatures in the 40s, snow slowly began to fall. It was a light snow, not the wet stuff of a March storm or the extra-light puffiness that can be blown by winds into a blizzard.

The air still seemed mild as I stepped outside to have a look. With a relatively light coat on and inadequate footwear, for I planned to go no farther than Karnell Street where I lived, I began walking, and walking. Down Karnell, right on State Street, left on Hillcrest, quick jog across the street to Locust, right on Hempstead to Brick Church, past the cemeteries and the church and Pete Erickson's land, left on Route 306.

I would eventually take Viola and Eckerson Roads back home, walking for a few hours in what seemed to be an even pace, driven as if by a motor within.

I thought of many things on this solitary walk, seeing only two cars and no people. The future was on my mind: studies, a job some day doing something (I thought then as a teacher). My parents and brother. Whether I would marry someday and have children.

While these heavy thoughts hit me at all angles, I became increasingly calm as I walked, and I now believe that this was on purpose, directed by a power that sets up all of our lives.

In looking back on that walk, which did not tire me though it was long, which was not difficult though a light snowstorm was constant, I can see that I began to notice even more deeply the woods, the houses, the roads, the many things that I now have the privilege to reflect on in my columns and in editorials in this newspaper.

I particularly recall seeing the old Halloran Brown fruit cold storage barn at Route 306 and Viola and the big "H.H. Brown" sign. I stood in the middle of Route 306 for a long time looking at the large building, which seemed to grow out of the slight rise off the southwest corner of the Route 306-Viola Road intersection.

There was something most sturdy about that building, and though I did not at that time define the meaning, it represented a steadiness that I have found in this land and its traditions.

I came home refreshed, renewed, ready to move ahead. There would be many, many mistakes ahead, much regret, some sterling moments and memories, some awfully fine people, and I would at times question whether that walk in the snow in February 1962 was only a teaser or a real glimpse into what can be the "heaven" of one's life, its essential meaning.

In all my doubts, I have now come to know that the door opened that night to a truth that it is my being. On the fresh, new snow, the great quiet of my life was secured, and it is from this place that I write.
(Aug. 27, 2002)

Of chicken soup and candy

The rain was heavy as the young woman walked into the diner with her small daughter. The child, oblivious to protocol because a 4-year-old has not yet set up too many rules and regulations in its more trusting world, rushed ahead of her mom as the two headed for the booth just behind mine.

Testing her seat for comfort by bouncing in it, the youngster asked – no, insisted – that she have a chocolate sundae with French fries and a pickle on the side.

The mother, because she is of the grownup world, knew that 10 a.m. was not the right time for a sundae and that there could never be a correct moment for a combination of ice cream, French fries and a pickle.

Besides, the mother and daughter were there, on this rainy day, for chicken soup. Each obviously had a cold, although the mother seemed to be suffering more. Chicken soup was to help alleviate the discomfort and the mother wanted both relief for her daughter and to teach a lesson, too. After all, she might have her own children someday, or want to offer someone else an age-old remedy.

Two bowls of soup were ordered, with two additional containers to go. The trip home, in the rain, might necessitate a booster shot.

As the soup was spooned delicately by the mother and slurped with delight by the daughter, another turn was noted in the lively conversation between the two. The daughter had been chattering away about the record-selection machine, the lights, the people, the floor, the food, the waitresses and everything else that entered her hungry, inquisitive mind and lingered for that brief moment that childhood inquiry allows.

Now it was the mother's chance to take the floor, to speak something serious to her daughter. The subject, naturally, was chicken soup and why it is good for you. Grandmothers' names were mentioned, ancient recipes were cited and stories of rapid improvement were told, all in an effort to lay the groundwork for the passing from mother to daughter of tradition.

The daughter looked wide-eyed as the mother intoned heritage, but also fidgeted, fixed her attention on other matters and finally broke off the conversation with the question, "Can I have a Peppermint Patty?"

"Yes," the mother said. "You can have a Peppermint Patty, but only if you finish your chicken soup." Somewhere, in that little girl's memory will forever lie a connection between chicken soup and the candy Peppermint Patty. That should only add to the legend.
(December 3, 1983)

Opening a tin with a 'key'

One of the best things about Fridays in my house in the 1950s was when my father would come home from grocery shopping. This was the time when sixth-graders like myself or my brother, Craig, would sit on the floor of the kitchen, across from the back door of the house in Hillcrest, and our father, who did the shopping because my mom didn't drive and worked during the day, would put the grocery bags on the floor.

Then he would roll the cans of vegetables, etc., to my brother or me, so we could put them in the cupboards.

We would also be sure to grab onto the lemon cookies that were my favorite, with this new supply almost devoured after I came home from the regular Friday night Troop 13 Boy Scout meeting at the Dutch Reformed Church in Spring Valley.

My father also would bring sliced American cheese from Charlie's Market in Nanuet, vanilla fudge ice cream for my brother (his favorite) and the fruits that my mother wisely insisted we should eat.

Fridays were always a time of bounty in my house, as is resupply anywhere, in peace and war. It must have been that way when the World War II military got fresh, hot chow, rather than rations, as the action on the front eased up.

Or when you cash your paycheck and add a little more to the plus side of your checking account.

Or when you meet a friend of long standing, and the two of you catch up.

Resupply time is good, no matter what or when it is.

A particularly memorable moment in grocery restocking in my house was when we opened up the coffee. I did not yet drink java in those young days, although I had some classmates who did, but I sure liked the terrific aroma of a newly opened can of ground beans.

This was my job, opening the can.

As my father rolled the Chase & Sanborn or Maxwell House to me, I eagerly awaited, putting it on the counter, turning it over to get the soldered "key" on the bottom of the six-inch-wide can, locating the tin tab on the side and winding the seam open with the key.

211

You would do that awfully slowly at first, sticking your nose close to catch the first sniff of vacuum-packed aroma. Then you had to be careful to unwind the seam straight, or you would have to get a pair of pliers to finish the job.

The room would fill with the smell of coffee just as my mother would walk in the door at the end of her work week, ready to put on another pot of fresh coffee for her friend and neighbor Irene Pfeffer.

Thus the weekend would begin for us in the old house on Karnell Street in the 1950s. Resupplied for the next seven days, and in a very real way, for life. (March 2, 2004)

Sampling N.J.'s woods

Took a walk the other day in Jersey woods. Not the same as Rockland woods.

You could bring me to a wooded area in this county, blindfold my bald head and transport me to nearby Jersey trees, and I would know I was not in the old neighborhood.

And this is said with the two woods in question just nine miles apart, from Chestnut Ridge to Fair Lawn.

Beautiful woods in both places, accessible from paved public trails in each location. Courteous walkers on both sides of the state line. A mix of similar trees, from the rare white birch to the usual maples and oaks. Streams, marshland in each spot, too.

So why is one park different from the other? Probably for the same reason that Westwood, in New Jersey, just five miles from Pearl River, is not like that hamlet at all.

It's as if you buy a sandwich of bologna and swiss in two delicatessens, and each tastes different, though the cold cuts and bread are from the same vendor. The taste is in the slicing, the way the cold cuts are placed on the bread, the finesse of the sandwich maker.

And, of course, you bring a mindset to each delicatessen. You feel a certain way in one that you do not in the other, and this colors your total perception.

So it must be in the two woods in question.

Reminds me of a story The Journal News once wrote about the old Goodman family out of the Spring Valley area. The couple had a beautiful, custom-built home off Scotland Hill Road in what is now Chestnut Ridge but which was then called south Spring Valley.

When they retired after many years of living in the house, they moved north, taking the original architectural plans and having the same home built so they would be familiar with everything.

And where was that house constructed? Well, in Rockland, Maine, of course.

Yet the two sites were not exactly the same, though the comfortable armchair was still next to the reading lamp, in a home that looked identical inside and out.

The Goodmans, happy as they were in each location, knew full well that they were now in Maine and not in south Spring Valley.

Must be the same way with the woods in Jersey and Rockland. There is something almost intangible in the unique perception that you get in each park.

For me, one was a nice place to visit, but the other was where I'd plant my feet for a longer stay.

(January 6, 2004)

'Relevance' of local history

History is relevance as well as relevant. What's history to one is yesterday's news to another or ancient times to a third person. It is what's *relevant* to you.

This writer has an interest in Rockland history and in the history of humankind — its themes, its standards, most of all its characters — and the hope is I that I relate to some of that in my weekly <u>column</u>.

Every once in a while, someone asks me to define Rockland history, particularly in the century just past. I am no expert on county history in any of its three centuries (we are now into the fourth). I'll leave that to people like the 19th century writers Dr. Frank B. Green and the Rev. David Cole, and the numerous historians of the 20th, including present County Historian Thomas F.X. Casey, Clarkstown Historian Bob Knight, Ramapo Historian Craig Long, Orangetown Historian Mary Cardenas, village historians like Win Perry of Upper Nyack, Gardner Watts of Suffern and Bob Goldberg of Nyack, Camp Shanks Historian Scott Webber and the Wilfred Talmans, Cordelia Bedells and Virginia Parkhursts of the mid-20th century.

Mostly, I can relate anecdotal history, since I am given a brain (maybe cursed with one) that remembers seemingly insignificant details of long ago. For whatever odd reason, I can still recall conversations uttered, say, on a Sunday afternoon in October 1962 when my friend and I were approaching Adele Boulevard, off New Hempstead in what is now the village of that name.

Somehow, the conversation is remembered as if it it is now being uttered because my brain "taped" it in the moment, relating it back in 1962 to passing a side street off a bigger road. I recall the moment today every time I pass the intersection.

Odd, but this sort of memory gives me colorful references for subjects in this column. Back to historical relevance: One of today's senior citizens who may have moved here in the second great suburban wave of the early 1960s may think he or she practically wrote 20th century Rockland history.

And that is half true, for anyone arriving on these shores in the early 1960s, or in the 1950s for that matter, forged a new county, taking it from a semi-rural farming community with specific downtowns and some key industry to suburban housing developments, shopping strips, changing politics, two interstates and highways and byways ever more connected to Gotham.

That is history, part of Rockland's history, and history that is *relevant* to the people who moved to Rockland 40-50 years ago. A different sort of history is relevant to Gene Erickson, the retired Hillcrest and then Monsey auto dealer (Oldsmobile, Toyota), whose father Clarence "Pete" Erickson was a longtime dairyman and Ramapo councilman.

He was the product of the old Spring Valley High School, and like the other high schools in Rockland in the 1930s, '40s and '50s, SVHS graduated classes of students who maintain lifelong, well-cemented relationships built on school sports, community doings, a small town.

George Chalsen, a Nyack High grad in the 1940s, will tell you the same thing, for before the suburban push, every family seemed to know every other family in Nyack — in the Valley, in Haverstraw, Suffern, Piermont, etc.

For such people, their history brings a different relevance, one forged by two or more generations of living in Rockland. It is impossible to say which history is more important, because, again, there is personal relevance. Each history carries its own frame of reference, its own memories, its particular characters, its standards, even its prejudices.

One of the great things about this Rockland is that there have always been quite diverse histories, because, since our beginning, existing so close to the Port of New York, we have a had a continuing mix of peoples with varied backgrounds. So, Rockland does not have just one history; it has many, each relevant to somebody or some group.

(Nov. 11, 2003)

With hope and a standard (The first column, 1981)

I've put the cart before the horse, as an old fool would. Or, maybe it's been a testing of the waters. Perhaps I've even been trying to walk on the water.

Whatever the case, I've given birth – I've tried to legitimize the outpouring of my soul, or at least what comes from my brain, through my fingers, to the typewriter (strike that, video display terminal).

In shorter terms, my column, to which you have been subjected in the past few weeks, now has a name – The Column Rule. It is a term of hidden meaning. In the newspaper business, especially in the old-time composing room among the printers, a column rule was a line of lead about 1/12 of an inch thick. Cut to the height of the other type, it was placed between columns to set them apart. Nowadays, few newspapers use column rules. An exception is The New York Times, which was reluctant to change its traditional typography when it went to "cold type," or photo composition, a few years ago.

For The Times, the column rule has had added meaning, as I hope the name will in my columns. If a Front Page story were set "indented," or with more white space between the columns so the column rule could be dropped, that meant, ever so subtly, that the piece was a feature, in-depth or otherwise. This may seem obscure to some readers, but to The Times it was the conservative, traditional, respectable way to differentiate a feature from the regular Front Page news stories. The column rule, or its absence, spoke for the newspaper.

When all newspapers used column rules, the printer, God bless his ink-covered soul, was king. Many smaller newspapers, in fact, left inside page makeup to these devils because of the intricacy and accuracy involved. They just didn't lay down a column rule using a printed line on cellophane tape as today's cold type paste-up people can do. They had to work with various lengths of lead strips, mitered pieces and type blocks in a craftsmanship that will be soon forgotten.

All this lead had to be placed in a form or "chase" – ever so carefully – before it was "locked up" and slid on a "turtle" so it could be brought to a roller press and a "mat" (or mold of the page) made in cardboard-like material. The mat was then used to make castings for the presses.

Column rules are easier to use today, yet they are used less. Whether this means quality – or at least a craft – has suffered, or whether the reverse is true – that the reader has benefited from a freer page style, I'll leave to the local debating society. All I know is that the column rule required some effort and the result was worth some pride.

With a certain degree of immodesty, I'll stick my neck out and hope my column, "The Column Rule," performs in like manner as did its namesake – that is, that it require some effort and is worth some pride. I will, I hope, speak as the column rule did – of tradition and craft, of the values of the old and of the necessity of maintaining standards in a topsy-turvy world of which Rockland is a small but important part.

(August 22, 1981)

INDEX

Ackerson, Wally, 113
Adele Boulevard, 215
Airmont, 114, 155, 183
Airmont Road, 153
"Alice in Wonderland"
  (movie), 129
Allied Radio, 95
Alpine, 91, 92
Alzheimer's disease,
  200
Andersen, Gerd
  Bitten, 67
Anderson, Maxwell, 17
André, Major John,
  49, 107
Apgar, Keith, 25
Appelbaum, Laura, x
Apples, 77
Army Air Corps, 185
Arnold's
Luncheonette, 57
Association of
  Vocational Education
  and Extension Boards,
  32
Athelstane Lodge,
  F.&A.M., 32
Attics, 81

Babe Ruth, viii
Bacall, Lauren, 61
Bader's, 101
Baker, Norman R.,
  11, 12, 13, 43, 57, 58
Bakeries, 165
Ball, Jim, 28
Ball family, 27
Ball, Tom, 28
Balogh, John, 9, 10
"Bambi" (movie), 129
Bartero's, 64

Battle of the Bulge, 187
Bauman's, 101
Bear Mountain, 113
Bear Mountain Inn,
  191
Beard, Daniel, 42
Beatty, Warren, 130
Bedell, Cornelia F.,
  51, 215
Benny, Jack, 195
Bernard, Josef, 68
Blauvelt, 164, 175
Booth, Carl, 35, 36
Booth family, 35
Boulevard, The,
  viii, 69, 101
Boy Scouts of America,
  42
Boy Scout Troop
  13, 211
Bradley Parkway, 85
Breslin, Jimmy, 171
Briarcraft Smoking
Pipe factory, 54, 73, 163
Brick Church, 41, 206
Brick Church
  Cemetery, 42
Brick Church section,
  31
Brick industry, 51, 105
Broadway (Nyack),
  3, 33, 57, 59
Broat, Mark, 83
Bronx, The, viii
"Brotherhood The,"
  119
Burghardt, Robert, 27
Butt, Tring, 83

Cable TV, 96
Cacioppo, Nancy, 39

Camp Hill School, 61
Camp Shanks,
  49, 51, 99, 100
Campbell's tomato
  soup, 87, 175
Canada, 79
Cardenas, Mary, 215
Carleton, Sir Guy, 49
Casey, Thomas F.X., xi,
  215
Catskills, The, ix, 101
Central Avenue
  (Spring Valley), 53, 74
Central Ford, 53
Central Highway
  (Haverstraw), 123
Central Nyack, 175
Chalsen, George, 216
Charlie's Market, 211
Chase & Sanborn
  coffee, 211
Chelsea-on-Hudson, 37
Cherry Lane, 155
Chestnut Ridge, 77,
  158, 213
Chevrolet, 27
Chicken soup, 209
Christmas, 117
Christmas cards, 117
Church St. (Spring
  Valley), 15, 69, 114
"Clarence," 29
Clarkstown, 115
Clarksville Inn, 114
Clausland Mountain,
  175
Clotheslines, 183
Coffee, 169
Colandrea, Frank,
  ("Martio"), 63
Colandrea, Lois, 63, 64

219

Cole, Rev. David, 51, 215
College Road, 103
Column rule, 217, 218
Comfort Coal, 74
Commerce St. (Spring Valley), 74
Committee for the Incorporation of the Village of Pomona, 61
Congregation Sons of Israel, 15
Concklin's orchards, 111
Consolidated Edison, 80
Couch, the, 13, 14
Crosby, Everett, 124
Crosfield Avenue, 113
Currier & Ives, 117
Custard crumb cakes, 165

Daily News, 38
Danish pastry, 166
Davenport, Tony, 171
Davis, Sandy, 83
D-Day, 99, 203, 204
DeBaun family, 35
Delaware tribe (of Indians), 89
Department of Transportation, 29
DePasquale, Coach, 35
Dexter Co., 5
Dickerman, Andrew, 13
D'Loughy, George, 21, 22, 83, 125
Donnellan, Jerry, 7, 8, 114
Drake's truck, 182
Drotch Motors, 27
Dutch Reformed Church, 211
Dutchtown, 29

Egelston, Col. Gerald, 5
Elliot's Luncheonette, 57
Ellis Island, viii, 101
Empire State Building, 95
Englewood (N.J.) News, 4
Erickson, Clarence E. ("Pete"), 31, 32, 206, 216
Erickson, Gene, 216
Erickson, Martha ("Marty"), 31
Erickson Dairy, 41
Erie Canal, 151
Erie Railroad, 74, 107, 109, 127, 151, 157
Ethlas Press Co., 33
Fair Lawn, 213
Family man, 179
Fazio, Rocco, 25, 26
Flieger, Holly, x
"First Lady of the American Stage," 59
Ford, ix
Four Corners, 113, 114
French bread, 166
"Front Page" (play and movie), 171

Galbreath family, 111
George Washington Bridge, vii, 91, 119
German- Americans, 39
Gettysburg, 193, 194
Glacial Age, 127
Goldberg, Bob, 215
Goodman family, 213
Good Samaritan Hospital, 41
Gram, Torger, x,
Grand Concourse, viii

Grand Concourse Hotel, The, viii
Grandparents, 195, 196
Grand View, 19, 20
Grassy Point Road, 105, 106
Great Depression, 81, 199
"Greatest Generation," 185
Green, Dr. Frank B., 51, 215
Grocery store clerk, 177
"Guns of Navarone" (movie), 130
Gunther, Andrew Edward, x, 197
Gunther, Arthur 4th, x, 197
Gunther, Arthur Jr., 42, 55, 56, 163
Gunther, Arthur Sr., 54, 73, 74, 114, 163, 187
Gunther, Craig, 21, 35, 55, 56, 74, 87, 129, 199, 211
Gunther family, 163
Gunther, Isabella Frances, 164
Gunther, Lillian, x, 164, 197
Gunther, Maud, 163
Gunther, Patricia, x, 44, 199, 200
Gunther, Winfield A., 187, 188

Hackensack, 165
Hackensack River Valley, 85
Hadeler, George W. Jr., 23, 24

Hadeler, George W. Sr., 23

Hadeler, George W. III, 23

Hadeler, Paul, 23

Halloran Brown, fruit cold storage barn, 206

Hammonton, N.J., 4

Hanging wash as social occasion, 183

Hanukkah, 117

Harniman, Kenneth F., 185

Haverstraw, 17, 29, 119, 216

Haverstraw Bay, 123

Haverstraw brick industry, 51

Haverstraw Times, 29

Hayes, Helen (Mrs. Charles MacArthur), 3, 59, 60

Hecht, Ben, 171

Hempstead St., 206

Henry Kulle, Inc., 27

Herald-Tribune, The, 38

Hickory Hill, 50

High Tor, 17, 18, 123

"High Tor" (play), 17

"High Tor" (movie), 61

High Tor beacon, 123

High Tor Farm, 17

High Tor Vineyards, 17, 123

Highview School, 115

Hi-Ho tavern, 37, 38

Hillburn, 127

Hillcrest, viii, ix, 47, 53, 69, 87, 96, 101, 129, 166, 183, 200, 205, 211, 216

Hillcrest Hotel, viii, 101

Historical Society of Rockland County, The, x, xi

"History of Rockland County, N.Y.," by Rev. David Cole, 51, 215

"History of Rockland County, The," by Dr. Frank B. Green, 51, 215

Hitler, Adolf, 99

Hoboken, N.J., 115

Hogan, Billy, 122

Hogan's Diner, 121

Ho-Ho-Kus, 165

Hotels, 101

Hollywood, 203

"How Things Began in Rockland County and Places Nearby," by Cornelia F. Bedell, 51

Hudson Ave. (Nyack), 13, 19, 57

Hudson River, 4, 19, 20, 30, 38, 60, 92, 106, 113

Hudson, Bob, 197

Huertgen Forest, 193, 203

Hunter College, 205

Hurley family, 111

Huts, 87

I-287, 92

Ice Age, 103

"Indian, The," 17, 18

Indian artifacts, 89

Indian campsites, 89

Indian Point, 154

International Ladies Garment Workers Union, 48

Irish-Americans, 39

Iraq war, 167, 193

"It's a Wonderful Life" (movie), 29

"Jack Benny Show" (television show), 81

Jackson, Betty, 42

Jackson, Carolyn, 42

Jackson, Gene, 41, 42, 83

Jackson, Harry, 41, 42, 68

Jackson, Harry Jr., 41, 42

Jewish people, 101

Jewish temple, Nanuet, 115

Jobson, Grant, ix, 11, 12, 14, 29, 37, 62, 171

Journalists, 37

Journal News, ii, vii, ix, x, xi, 3, 5, 4, 11-13, 19, 33, 39, 43, 44, 51, 57, 61, 89, 113, 121, 185, 186, 205, 213

Kakiat, 157

Kalinin, Xenia, xi

Kapunan, Patricia, x

Karnell St., 47, 53, 87, 205, 212

Knight, Bob, 215

Koerner, Bill, 17, 29, 30

Korean War, 7

Korvette's, 79, 113

Krug's driver, 182

Kulle, Edward, 27

Kulle, Henry, 27, 28

Kuperman Cape Cods, 47

Ladentown, 85

Lafayette Ave. (Suffern), 109

Lafayette Theatre, 109, 129

Lawrence St. (Spring Valley), 9, 27, 74, 95

Lederle Laboratories, 79, 199
Lenik, Edward J., 89, 90
Lenni-Lenapi Indians, 127
Levenson, Joel, 117
Levitt family, 81
Levy, Eugene, 31, 32
Lincoln, Abraham, 194
Litter, 85
Little Tor, 17
Locust St. (Hillcrest), 69, 205
Loh, Jules, x
Logue, John ("Butch"), 33, 34
Logue, Mae, 33
Long, Craig, 215
Low Tor Mountain, 79
Lutheran church, Nanuet, 115
Lyons, John, 199
Lyons, Mary, 199
Lyons, William, 199

Mabie's Tavern, 49
Mahwah River, 109
MacArthur, Charles, 171
MacArthur, Gen. Douglas, 194
Madawick family, 111
Madison Ave. (Spring Valley), 15
Magers' general store, 177
Main Line/Port Jervis line, 109
Main St. (Nyack), 3, 33, 37
Main St. (Spring Valley), 15, 21, 27, 64, 69, 74

Majestic Barbershop, 9, 10
Man, Albon, x
Manse (Tappan), 108
Maple Ave. (Spring Valley), 74
Marine Midland Bank, 33
Markow, Mrs., 53
Marsilio, George, 37, 38
Marsilio, John E., 37, 38
"Martio," 63, 64
Martio's Pizza Parlor, 63, 64
Masons, 32
Marx, Groucho, 81
Maxwell House coffee, 211
Mazzeppa Engine Co., No. 2, 33
Medal of Freedom, 59
Melone, Betty, 49, 50
Melone, Paul, 49, 50
Memorial Park (Spring Valley), 21, 125
Meredith, Burgess, 61, 62
Milkmen, 181
Middletown Road, 115
Minestrone soup, 175
Mission style/ Craftsman/ Stickley furniture, 163
Monday Morning Quarterback Club, 79
Monsey, 114, 153, 155, 157, 205, 216
Monsey bungalows, 157
Monsey Glen, 90, 157
Montgomery Ward, 96
Montvale, 166

Mount Ivy, 62
Munsee Indians, 89, 157, 158
Mussolini, Benito, 99

Nanuet, 64, 79, 114, 115, 151, 153, 200, 211
Nanuet Hotel, 63, 115
Nanuet Mall, 115
Nanuet Restaurant, 63, 115
New Amsterdam, 51
New Antrim, 109
New City, vii, 17, 107, 113, 115
New Hempstead, 215
New Jersey's woods, 213
New York City, 79, 80, 83, 92
New York City firefighters, 119
New York City police officers, 119
New York State Department of Transportation, 152
New York State Publishers Association, 58
New York State Thruway, 5, 20, 89, 91, 92, 102, 113, 127, 153
New York Times, The, 217
New York, West Shore and Buffalo Railroad, 107
Newspapers, 171
North Main Street School, viii, x, 25, 55, 101
Northern Railroad, 107

"Now and Then and Long Ago in Rockland County," by Cornelia F. Bedell, 51
Nurturing children, 173
Nyack, 3, 4, 19, 33, 37, 43, 57, 59, 79, 91, 109, 114, 175, 185, 216
Nyack Daily News, 3, 4, 11
Nyack Evening Journal, 4, 11, 19, 33, 51
Nyack ferry landing, 114
Nyack High School, 115, 186, 216
Nyack Hospital, 114
Nyack Selective Service Board, 203
Nyack Street Fair, 31
Nyack-to-Tarrytown ferry, 91
Nyack Turnpike, 109, 115

O'Donoghue's Tavern, 33
Old Reformed Church (Tappan), 108
Old 59, 113, 114
Old Nyack Turnpike, 53, 87, 114, 153
Olympic Track and Field Trials, 1936, 41, 42
Omaha Beach, 203
Oneonta (N.Y.) Star, 4
Orange & Rockland Utilities, 80
Orangeburg, 79, 99, 100, 153
Orange County, 107
Orangetown Patent, 107

Orangetown Resolutions, 107
Orangetown sewers, 43
Orangetown Telegram, 51
Orchard St. (Nanuet), 115
Ortner's, 101

Pacific campaign (World War II), 193
Palisades, 45, 46
Palisades Center Mall, 121
Palisades Free Library, 45, 46
Palisades Interstate Parkway, 5, 20, 91, 92, 102, 153, 156
Palisades Presbyterian Church, 45
Parkhurst, Virginia, 3, 4, 215
Pascack Valley Line, 115
Paterson (N.J.), 165
Pearl Harbor, 193
Pearl River, ix, 5, 23, 39, 79, 119, 183, 199, 200, 213
Pearl River Democratic Party, 40
Pearl River High School, 115
Pearl River Rotary Club, 40
"Pearl River Then and Now" by Herbert Peckman, 39
Peckman, Donald, 40
Peckman, Herb, ix, 39, 40
Peckman's Liquors, 40

"Penguin," 61
Peppermint Patty, 209, 210
Perruna, Vic, 125
Perruna's Pizza Parlor and Restaurant, 64, 125
Perry, Win, 215
Piermont, 107, 151, 216
Pipetown section (Spring Valley), 73
Plaza Restaurant, 31
Pomona, 61, 111
Pomona Country Club, 111
Pomona Road, 67, 153
Post family, 45
Potake Lake, 89
POW/MIA, 7
Prescott family, 111
Prescott, Joan, 67
Pyle, Ernie, 188

Quaker Rd., 61

Radio Association of Rockland, 79
Rail tunnel (in Orangetown), 152
Ramapo, 31
Ramapo Land Co., 89
Ramapo Mountains, 89, 103, 104, 111, 155
Ramapo River, 107, 127
Ramapo Town Council, 32
Ramapo Trust Co., 9
"Reflections," by Mildred Post, 45
Rickard-Meyer, Leland, 67, 84
Rickley, Harold, 53

Ridge Street
  (Spring Valley), 117
Rippey, Mildred Post,
  45, 46
Rittberg, Arnold, 47
Rittberg, Edith, 47
Rittberg, Matthew, 47
Rocking chair, 163
Rockland Community
  College, 45, 69, 103,
  153
Rockland County
  Evening Journal,
  3, 11
Rockland County
  Highway Department,
  152
Rockland County
  Sports Hall of Fame,
  186
Rockland County
  Times, 12
Rockland County
  Vocational and
  Guidance Board, 32
Rockland Hall of
  Fame, 42
Rockland Independent,
  51
Rockland Leader,
  31, 32, 51
Rockland Veterans
  of Foreign Wars, 186
Rockwell, Norman, 117
Ro-Field's Appliance
  Store, 15, 69
Romaine, John Sr.,
  15, 16, 68, 69, 70,
  114, 117
Romaine, John Jr., 70
Romaine, Lucille,
  70, 83, 114
Romaine, Marie,
  68, 70, 114

Roth's store, 177
Route 9W,
  29, 91, 105, 155
Route 17, 89, 127
Route 45, 111
Route 59, 67, 73,
  90, 92, 105, 106, 109,
  113, 153, 155, 157
Route 202,
  105, 109, 155
Route 303, 155, 156
Route 304, 155
Route 306, 111,
  156, 157, 206
Rouy, Amy, 54, 117
Rouy, Helen, 54, 117
Royle, CynDee, x
Rubenfeld's, 101
Ruth, Babe, viii

Sacred Heart Church,
  109
Saddle River, 155
Saddle River Road, 157
St. Joseph's Church,
  15, 64
Savell, Isabelle, 19, 20
"Saving Private Ryan"
  (movie), 203
"Schmatte," 191
School District No. 8,
  32
Scotland Hill Road,
  213
Sears, 96
Dr. Selman, 54
Seven Lakes Drive, 153
'76 House, 49
Servicemen and
  women, 167
Shelly, Joe, 125
Sherwood family, 35
Sickletown Road, 151
Singer's, 101

Sloatsburg, 127,
  183, 200
Smith Road, 85
Snedens Landing, 107
Soloveitchik, Rabbi
  Josef, 15, 16
Sound Radio, 95
Soups, 176
South Broadway
  (Nyack), 19
South Main Street
  School, 12, 25,
  54, 55, 117
South Mountain
  Road, viii, 123, 189
South Nyack, 20, 91, 92
South Orangetown, 45
South Orangetown
  School District,
  54, 197
Sparkill, 85, 107
Spielberg, Steven, 203
"Splendor in the
  Grass" (movie), 130
Spring Valley, viii,
  ix, x, 9, 10, 15,
  16, 21, 25, 27, 31,
  35, 36, 53-55,
  63, 64, 68, 69, 73,
  85, 87, 95, 96,
  100-102, 109,
  114, 119, 125,
  129, 158, 163,
  177, 183, 187,
  191, 200, 211, 213
Spring Valley High
  School, 42, 55, 67, 68,
  83, 84, 115, 216
Spring Valley Junior
  High School, 26
Spring Valley post
  office, 117
State St. (Spring
  Valley), 205

224

Statue of Liberty, viii, 101
Stickley, Gustav, 163
Stony Point, 27, 85, 153
Stony Point Planning Board, 121
Strawberry Place Luncheonette, 57
Strippoli, Rosemarie, 53, 54
Strunck's store, 177
Suffern, 85, 92, 109, 110, 114, 127, 129, 216
Suffern Free Library, 109
Suffern, George, 110
Suffern, John, 109
Suffern Village Hall, 109
Sutter, John A. (Jack), 5, 6, 13, 14, 43, 44
Sutter, Evelyn, 44

Tallman, 114, 155, 156, 158, 183, 200
Tallman Ave. (Nyack), 3
Talma, Douwe Harmanse, 51
Talman, Peter, 51
Talman, Wilfred B., 51, 52, 215
Talman family, 35
Taplin, R. Clinton, 43
Tappan, 49, 50, 107
Tappan Landing, 107
Tappan Library, 50, 108
Tappan Slote, 107
Tappantown Historical Society, 50
Tappan Zee Bridge, vii, 5, 10, 19, 20, 91, 102, 105, 113

Tappan Zee Preservation Coalition, 20
Tarrytown, 91, 114
Ternure Ave. (Spring Valley), 73, 74, 96, 164
Thompson, Herbert, 55, 56
Tierney, Gene, 40
Tiger's Den, 125
"Tin Man" Triathlon, 197
"Tire King," 27, 28
Tires, 27
Tojo, 99
Tone, Franchot, 62
Torne Mountain, 127
"Town of Friendly People," 39
Travers, Henry, 29
Tupper Lake, 197
TV aerials, 95
TV channels, 95
Twin Ave. (Spring Valley), 35

Union Road (Spring Valley), 129
Upper Nyack, 33
Utah Beach, 203

Valley Theater (Spring Valley), 129
Van Huysen, Hermanus, 108
Van den Hende, Jana H., 61
Van Orden, Elmer, 17, 18
Versailles, 99
Vietnam, 7, 8, 167, 168

"Village of the Dammed" (movie), 129
Viola, 85, 104, 157, 158, 205, 206
Viola Road, 85, 103, 206
Volk, Al, 3

Washington, Avenue, (Suffern), 109
Washington, Gen. George, 49, 107
Washington St. (Spring Valley), 10
Waters, Barney, 117
Watts, Gardner, 215
Webber, Scott, 215
Weissman, David ("Duvid"), 47, 48
Weissman, Molly, 47, 48
Weissman's, 101
Weltie, Gus, 17, 18
West New Hempstead Cemetery, 67, 68
West Nyack, 13, 19, 27, 43, 85, 113, 128, 175
West Nyack Road, 113
West Nyack Swamp, 203
Westwood, 213
White House, 59
Widmann's Bakery, 27
Wilkes, John, 17
Williams, Walter, 11, 12, 58
Wilson, President Woodrow, 99
Winter coat, 161
"Winterset" (play), 61
Witt, Al, 61

"Wizard of Oz, The"
  (movie), 117
Women's Army
  Corps (WACS), 4
Wood, Natalie, 130
Woodside Diary, 31
World Telegram &
  Sun , The, 38
World Trade Center,
  119, 193
World War I, 99, 193
World War II, 4,
  23, 99, 167, 185,
  187, 203, 204

Yankee Stadium, viii
Yatto, Fred Sr., 68
Yatto, Fred Jr., 67, 68
Yatto, Robert, 68
Yatto, Selma, 68
Yatto, Thomas, 68
Yeager Health Center,
  200
Yiddish, 15, 47, 191
Yonkers, 91
"You Bet Your Life"
(television show), 81

Zaun, Lt. Jeffrey N., 7
Zimmer's store, 177

www.ingramcontent.com/pod-product-compliance
Lightning Source LLC
Chambersburg PA
CBHW080700110426

42739CB00034B/3340